Irreverence, scurrility, profanity, vilification and licentious abuse:

MONTY PYTHON
THE CASE AGAINST

Robert Hewison

GROVE PRESS, INC., NEW YORK

First Evergreen Edition 1981
First Printing 1981
ISBN: 0–394–17949–8
Library of Congress Catalog Card Number: 81–47631

Manufactured in Great Britain

GROVE PRESS, INC.
196 West Houston Street, New York, N.Y. 10014

Contents

Cultural vandalism— that's all 'The Life of Brian' is

young Bette

But what 'Das
two young
'cream' of urn
to defend wh
vandalism. T
really very si
youngster
windows in
They do w
charm and en
and by it
sometimes
how many lischen Film.
would appla
young villa hm syn-
public garde sierte
bs and le Fassung
se w

Fuck Jesus?

Die englische Satiriker-
gruppe Monty Py-
hon's Flying Circus
oduzierte einen
lischen Film.
hm syn-
sierte
le Fassung
ider

y
end
k in
o the
a there
o show
breaking
l the same,
e fourth and
our era have
tehat today we
ten and bus
dalised.
s Her he Oxford
h in dee has to do
an »die "a wilful or
of anything
anderen, worthy of
je. h a person is
uncultured.
liam Buckle destruction or
d die Python-g beautiful or
nierte, ob wir wo
Geschmacklosi or
witz, wo die Dars ppers, von Anne
Mamba-Schritt in die Gaskam
haben. (Daß seine Landsleu
chau auf Erinnerungsfotos —
bannen, ist ihm wohl bisher
r ist dieser *Brian*, der so heiß
*John Cleese, her med fuldskæg
d'Angleterre. Skranken og anta
hotel i den sydengelske badeby
til sit værelse.*

touch with their cultural
heritage. In fact, products of
our oldest universities add to
the quota of vandal
accept the diction
about "destruct
of anything th
venerable"
of the fil
In the o
carr

Du sérieux... ...dans la folie

Dur labeur que d'interviewer les Monty Python. D'abord, ils
sont six et déferlent sur vous comme un raz de marée.
parlent vite, rient, font des apartés bl
en récréation. Le grand s
s'anime à leu

Descriptions match

When I lived in Oregon, I had friends, a couple.
She was a refugee from the communists; he was a
veteran of World War II who had been stationed in
Africa. He told of a building that advertised as the
devil's church. Curiosity once led him within its
doors. His descriptions of the teachings could have
been lifted from what I have heard of the movie
"The Life of Brian."

This picture, that was written in Sweden,
financed I imagine by Russia and produced in
England, is nothing more or less than a proselyting
tool of the church of the devil. To attend it would be
tantamount to attending a witches' coven, only much
worse. I think if people really understood this, it
would die for lack of patronage. Heads of churches
and all Christians also have a call to make its real
purpose clear. If I were the church leaders I would
send spies to see who does attend.—Christie Pace,
Cecil.

vision. Graham Chap
aux lèvres, n'oublie
passé de docteur. A se
de loisirs, il compulse
et livres de médecine.
geant son temps entre L
et Hollywood où il vit si
par an, Graham achè
roman, *L'Autobiographie*
menteur et le script c
comédie d'aventure,
curieux travail une histoir
pirate qu'il espère interpr
bientôt aux Etats-Unis.
chael Palin, comédien, par
cipe à de nombreuses
sions télévisées, s'occupe de
femme et de ses deux enfants.

Apparences trompeuses
Derrière le masque de « gu-
gusse » se cachent sérieux et
profondeur. Les Monty Python
ne sont pas de grands gaill-
écervelés, des
core

inée, ils
ketches,
lurons
jet est
rammé.
as en-
urs oc-
côté.
une
itan-
hau-
n de
sa
la
res
ur

Humo

John Cleese fra M

Af Eva Schulsinger
PUBLIKUM TROR, at vi
rer os gevaldigt og improvi
på livet los, men alt er tim
planlagt i mindste d
holder os strikt til
skript. Det er egentl
ligt, fortæller den 1
40-årige englænder
fra Monty Pythons
cus. Også kendt som
vanlige vært i Halle
hotellet.

Han er i øjeblikke
Danmark, men gav i
møde med pressen, f
mere lidt for de gale
res nye film. Et H
som får premiere i
den 25. august.

— Jeg bryder mig
om at filme. Man sk

l
C
å
sa
l'é
me
et
sa
Cecil.

Zwei „Monty Pythons" in Hamburg

Jungs, ist euch denn gar nichts heilig?

Sie haben Phantasie, Witz, Mut, inzwischen auch et-
was Mammon und ein Publikum, das sich vor ihnen
glatt auf den Boden wirft — vor Lachen. Nur eines haben sie nicht: Respekt. Englands zur Zeit wohl be-
rühmteste Komikergruppe, „Monty Python", erntet für
ihren jüngsten Spielfilm „Das Leben des Brian" in Paris, London und New York schon seit Wochen laute

I

Introduction

'Censorship has become a very emotive word – almost the dirtiest word in the English language.'
Mrs Mary Whitehouse

This is a book about censorship. It sets out, not so much to attack censorship, as to describe how it has operated over the last ten years in relation to a particular group of people, the creators of *Monty Python's Flying Circus*. In Western societies formal censorship is itself formally limited, but there are other ways in which the expression of ideas is controlled. Beside the open activities of boards of film censors, and the statutory restrictions of the law, must be set the institutional censorship of large organizations and the commercial censorship of companies that refuse to produce or market the means by which ideas are conveyed.

The operation of institutional and commercial censorship is more insidious than the open censorship of the law, for it usually takes place unnoticed: the path of the blue pencil is erased, because with its passage the object of censorship also disappears. Ideas are struck out before they have a chance to be developed, or even of being known about by more than their creator and their censor. Even if the idea reaches communicable form, it may be so altered by those who control the means of communicating it as to be worthless in the creator's eyes. Such censorship is also much harder to detect, for there are many reasons why an idea can be turned down as unacceptable, unproducible or unmarketable. That is why there exists a fourth category of control: self-censorship. Those who have ideas they wish to communicate are continually adjusting them in the light of what they believe they can or cannot do. Some ideas never get further than the inside of their creator's head, for the creator knows that it would not be worth the personal (or financial) frustration to try to take the idea any further. Other ideas are shaped and modified by pressures to which the creator must concede, even if it means that what appears is only an approximation of what was originally intended.

Censorship, like creation, is dynamic rather than static, and is highly responsive to the mood of the times. It varies in intensity between one country and another, and from area to area even within a country as small as the United Kingdom. It varies according to the medium through which the ideas are expressed. The word enjoys a more privileged position than the image, for words in a book are considered to be less of a threat than pictures in a magazine, but the spoken word on television is censored more heavily than the word on a printed page. Images in a single painting, mass produced images in a book, moving images on a film screen, moving images on television are treated differently because of their different social context, though the action depicted may be exactly the same. Censorship varies in intensity over questions of sex, violence, religion and politics. But censorship is important, for when, however shakily, a society draws the line between what can and cannot be said, it is drawing the line that defines the boundary of its own culture. In the 1960s in Britain and the United States those boundaries appeared to be widening; in the 1970s and 1980s those boundaries have ceased to expand, and some people would like to see them contract.

Within these boundaries, people create. They may be deeply serious artists or, as in this case, sometimes no less serious comedians. The creators of *Monty Python's Flying Circus* have encountered formal, institutional and commercial censorship, and they have chosen at times to modify their ideas in the interest of getting them across to as wide an audience as possible. They do not feel that they have suffered any worse than others from censorship, but the point is that they have not suffered any less. Much censorship passes unnoticed because there is nothing there to be seen, and censors, when they give reasons at all, give them in private.

Monty Python: the Case Against is therefore presented not as a protest, but as a case history. Because the culture from which they sprang is distinctly British and all their work to date has a British base, this account focuses on the British experience of *Monty Python's* creators, though they have applied the same principles of resistance to censorship in all contexts. Their most important application of that principle was in the United States. By opening their records and files the makers of *Monty Python* have made it possible to show how censorship works: the formal rules they must obey, the informal pressures upon them. It is only when the details of what censorship means in practice are revealed that it is possible to decide whether or not its decisions are absurd. The Pythons have not told me what to say, and they have not censored this book.

TUBULAR STRUCTURE. ATTENDANT IN SHORTS TOO.)

And it's not just the modern so-called plastic
arts that gets the clean-up treatment.

CUT TO

INT. THEATRE STAGE (EALING???)
DESDEMONA ON BED. OTHELLO WITH HER)

OTHELLO
Oh Desdemona, Desdemona.

(THE PEPPERPOTS RACE ON TO THE STAGE AND PULL
HIM OFF)

PEPPERPOTS (TO DES)
Come on dear. Don't let that darkie touch you
...get back where you came from you coon etc...

(THE PEPPERPOTS START TO BEAT UP OTHELLO.)

And those continentals had better watch out for
their dirty foreign literature. Jean Paul Sartre
and Jean Genet won't know what's hit them.
Never mind the foulness of their language -
come '73 they'll all have to write in British.

(PEPPERPOTS BURNING BOOKS. NIGHT.)

"ORIGIN OF THE SPECIES" "RUPERT BEAR" "GUARDIAN"
"TEXTBOOK OF GYNAECOLOGY" "SARTRE" "DAS KAPITAL"
"PROUST" "BERTRAND RUSSELL" "PLATO" "MONTY
PYTHON'S BIG RED BOOK" "FREUD" "CRIMINOLOGY"
"SOCIOLOGY" "PRIVATE EYE" "P. WILDBLOOD".)

V.O.
And you can keep your fastidious continental
bidets Mrs Foreigner - Mrs Britain knows how to
keep her feet clean...

(GROUP OF PEPPERPOTS WAVING)

- but she'll battle like bingo boys when it
comes to keeping the television screen clean...

(CUT TO THE BEEB: TV CENTRE PULL BACK. THE
PEPPERPOTS ARE ALL PARADING AS COMMISSIONAIRES
WITH FASCIST OVERTONES... CHECKING PEOPLE'S
PAPERS)
SIGN SAYS: 'CLEAN TV CENTRE'
            'GOD SAYS NO TO FILTH'
            'TO THE CELLS'

ENORMOUS PHOTOS: QUEEN VICTORIA
                 SMITH
                 NIXON
        ONE MAN WEARING BOXER SHORTS OVER TROUSERS

IN BACKGROUND A SIGN: 'WANTED DEAD OR ALIVE'
PHOTO: ROBERT ROBINSON

Better watch out for those nasty continental
shows on the sneaky second channel too.
But apart from attacking that prurient hot-bed
of left-wing continentals at Shepherds Bush
what else do these ordinary mums think?

(TROOP OF PEOPLE BEING LED OUT SHACKLED
TOGETHER.)

V.O.
Do they accept the dialectical logic of latter
day Hegelianism?

P.POTS:
No.

II

'The best ideas must come from below'

Sir Hugh Greene

Monty Python's Flying Circus first appeared as the replacement for a religious programme. During the late 1960s BBC Television was in the habit of giving the religious discussion programme broadcast early on Sunday evenings a second showing much later that night. This was at the special request of clergymen who said that they were too busy to watch earlier in the day. But by August 1969 it was clear that few people, if any, were watching. The clergy now said they were too tired to watch at the end of their busiest day of the week, while the rest of the television audience still awake was watching commercial television's *The David Jacobs Celebrity Show*, in preference to Malcolm Muggeridge's interviews with religious worthies. So the religious repeat was moved to Tuesday, and the *Flying Circus* was cleared for take off.

As a result, *Monty Python* earned its first hostile editorial before it had even been seen on the screen. On 25 August the *Daily Telegraph* ticked off the BBC for its lack of taste in descending to concern about the ratings: 'Is this a sufficient reason for dropping that programme with glee, and substituting comedy shows which the BBC announces as "Nutty, zany and odd-ball"? Is this not yet another instance of the BBC's desire to forget, as far as it can, its subsidized status and its duty to maintain high standards, in order to compete for audience ratings with ITV?'

When *Monty Python* actually appeared for the first time, on 5 October, the *Telegraph*'s television critic, Norman Hare, was more amused: 'It could be that Messrs Cleese, Chapman, Jones, Palin and Idle, the writer-performers involved, will prove less soporific than Mr Muggeridge, if not as intelligent.' The comparison was put to the test almost exactly ten years later, when Mr Muggeridge and two representative Pythons met face to face for a late night television discussion. This book is about the controversy the Pythons provoked in the ten years in between.

The opening shows of *Monty Python's Flying Circus* proved anything but soporific. From the moment Gilliam's surrealist cartoon titles appeared to the confident march of Souza's 'Liberty Bell' you knew – in that quickly established catch-phrase – that you were in for something completely different. The printed word is an inefficient way of communicating the excitement of the speeding images on the screen. It was not just the rate at which ideas came and went during the show's half-hour, it was their rich absurdity and the blithe carelessness with which they were taken up and thrown away, which made the show so unusual. The writers seemed to have so many ideas that items which might have been stretched into a situation comedy were consumed in seconds in order to make room for more. All the gags were running gags because only at that pace could they all be fitted in.

It quickly became apparent that, although this show was nothing like the 'satirical' programmes that launched the new BBC TV comedy of the 1960s, *Monty*

THE SILLY PARTY

**The leader of the Silly Party
The Rt. Hon. Loopy X**

Support the Silly Party. The only party that is publicly committed to:

* raising prices
* destroying industry
* causing inflation
* ruining the economy

A Silly Government would:

* raise the school leaving age to 43
* encourage naughtiness in high places
* maintain confidence in British Silliness abroad

Python's Flying Circus was subversive. Television satire of the kind that relied on mimicking the external characteristics of politicians, but only rarely thrust a critical knife into their inner fraudulences, lost its force when it was realized that at least some politicians of the television age felt flattered by parodies that reinforced their own brand images. *Monty Python* went about it another way, by saying outrageous things in an outrageous context. Television is itself a form of authority, which is why it is (in emergent countries, literally) the most closely guarded medium. *Monty Python* subverted the idea of television. It had an obsession with the forms of TV programmes that went beyond the idea of parodying familiar names or faces or shows. Television credits, for instance, have always been the solemn demarcation points between one kind of programme and another, signals to the audience to adjust its perception, but *Monty Python* specialized in tearing that convention apart, putting the beginning at the end and the end at the middle, playing with continuity by using confusing station identification signs, sometimes from the rival channel.

Monty Python created its own mode of perceiving television, from the early weather report to the late-night religious epilogue. And, especially, it was subversive of the idea of television comedy itself. It threw away the idea of separate sketches with laboriously plotted punchlines in exchange for a tumbling stream of consciousness like a hilarious bad dream. They did not despise punchlines, if they were good ones, but they did not need them, for these were part of the old, exploded routine.

The great advantage of the *Flying Circus* was that the writers were also the performers, so that there was no halting gap between intention and execution. The performers knew exactly what the writers had imagined, for they were the same people, and the nuances which no typed script can convey, the voices, attitudes, the timing that dictates which line to play up and which to play down, were instinctively right. The team appeared in a bewildering series of roles, where the wigs, costume and make-up were as convincing as the mimicry of the voices. And just when invention would be expected to sag, the scene was transformed (without any loss of interior logic) into the world of Terry Gilliam's animations. It goes without saying that the material and performances were funny, but, without being heavy-handed in the old lampooning style, they were always funny *about* something, frequently about figures of authority. There was always a strong thread of contemporary critical comment in what they chose to be funny about.

Monty Python quickly became a cult. (Going out irregularly, late at night, with no promotion from the BBC, a minority cult is all that it could be.) Its energy and enthusiasm transmitted itself to the audience, who rejoiced in the absurdity of it all. It was no longer possible to take continuity announcers or Spam seriously, and the derangement of perception within the programme spread outwards to all television, most of all to television commercials, which have the same insistent attack as *Monty Python*, without the nonsense. Jokes, characters and catch-phrases became the secret signs of members of the cult, and the Pythons found their jokes replayed to them, as in these presents from fans or this dinner menu from a hotel where they stayed during filming. The great pleasure of Python was that while audience appreciation distinctly faded out above the age of thirty-five, there were many public figures – such as those who appeared fleetingly in shows, or were guyed in the Python books – who joined in the absurdities with enthusiasm. To use the word the Pythons have adopted, adapted and improved, it was all wonderfully silly.

Monty Python's Flying Circus was good because its individual members had served long apprenticeships writing and performing in other shows. Their entire professional experience was in television comedy, at a time when, starting with *That Was the Week That Was* in 1962, the form had become increasingly confident and challenging. One of the reasons for this is the evolution of the writer-performer, who (ideally) has the intelligence of the former and the authority of the latter. Such performers were very much the products of the unofficial schools of cabaret and revue that flourished at Oxford and Cambridge Universities in the early sixties and, excepting Gilliam, the Pythons were graduates from both. The five Britons then served in the regiment of writers and performers who contributed to the success of David Frost.

All aged between twenty-six and thirty in 1969, John Cleese, Graham Chapman and Eric Idle were from Cambridge, Michael Palin and Terry Jones from Oxford. At the beginning of 1969 Chapman and Cleese were working together as a script-writing team on such projects as the opening show of the *Doctor in the House* series. Palin, Jones and Idle were appearing in ITV's early evening programme, *Do Not Adjust Your Set*. Chapman and Cleese ended their working day on Wednesdays by watching *Do Not Adjust Your Set* and they enjoyed what they saw. Turning to Chapman at the end of one show, John Cleese said: 'It's time we did some more telly.' A meeting was arranged.

The first contact was between Cleese and Palin, who brought in his partner Jones; together they brought in Idle and the American cartoonist Terry Gilliam, who contributed animated sections to *Do Not Adjust Your Set*. Some years before Gilliam had featured Cleese in his short-lived New York magazine *Help!*, so the circle of contacts was closed. At first, everyone was cautious, and the group began as it has never left off, with extreme difficulty in finding a date, a time and a place where all six could meet. Early in May there was a

8

MENU

Chilled Spam Juices
Honeydew Spam
Smoked Spam
Cream of Spam Soup

***

Fillet of Spam Mornay

***

Grilled Spam Carni
Roast Gigot of Spam & Spam Sauce
Grilled Spam with Spam

COLD SPAM

Home Cooked Spam
Spam
Spam Salad
Roast Spam
Spam Spears

Spam Croquettes

***

Spam Flan
Spam Melba
Lemon Sorbet Spam
Strawberry Spam
Spam Board

***

Gaelic Spam

Spam House Hotel,
Stanmore,
5th October 1971.

curry lunch at the Light of Kashmir, Fleet Road, and a meeting on 11 May at Cleese's Basil Street flat, after a recording of *Do Not Adjust Your Set.* At no time was there any question but that this was to be a show for the BBC; their contacts and reputation there were good, and they had the important support of the writer and producer Barry Took, with whom they had worked on *The Frost Report.* Took was on the staff of the BBC, and sold the idea of a new show by a new team to the executives of the Light Entertainment department. On 23 May the Pythons gathered with Barry Took in a conference in the Television Centre. Michael Mills, the BBC's Head of Comedy, hurried in to announce that they would be commissioned to write and perform a thirteen-part series, and hurried out again. It was only the second time that all six had met in the same room.

It is well known that the group spent weeks arguing over what the show should be called (Terry Jones was keeping the notes at the meeting that finally decided it), but they also spent weeks arguing over everything else, and this has become the Python method. The Python team is a core of energy held together by its own opposing forces: there is still, after more than ten years' existence, a division of attitude between those who went to Cambridge and those who went to Oxford, a difference that stretches back to the time when they appeared in competing revues on the Fringe at the Edinburgh Festival. Terry Gilliam's totally different conditioning by the America of the mid-1960s cuts straight across these ancient rivalries. There are great differences of style and personality; the extreme opposition is between John Cleese – tall, English, Cambridge, a stereotype figure of authority turned inside out, but still retaining a respect for reason and order – and Terry Jones, shortish, Welsh, Oxford, warm, outgoing and highly volatile with a passionate commitment to getting things, as he sees them, right at all costs. John Cleese and Terry Jones are guaranteed to disagree on everything – but that does not mean that they cancel each other out. Instead, the one is a foil to the other, and each can be too dominant on his own.

There are other checks and balances, too, within the group. John Cleese may be tall, but he cannot dominate through height alone, for Graham Chapman is almost as big. In meetings Chapman has the important role of The One Who Stays Silent, though elsewhere he provides contrasts as the only homosexual, and for a long time he entertained and distracted the others as a terrible drunk. Eric Idle, the only member of the group who has always written on his own, is the acidic intellectual of the team, fastidious and cerebral in opposition to Terry Gilliam's anarchic joy in low-life and ordure. Eric Idle's Cambridge sharpness is smoothed by Michael Palin's Oxford amiability, and it is Michael Palin's good will that has placed him nearest

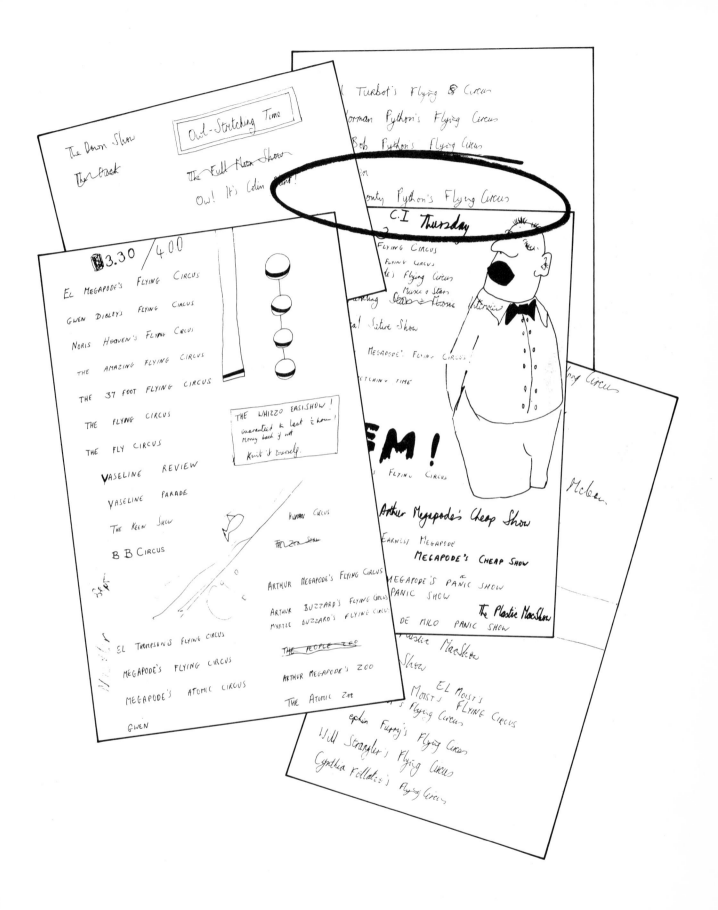

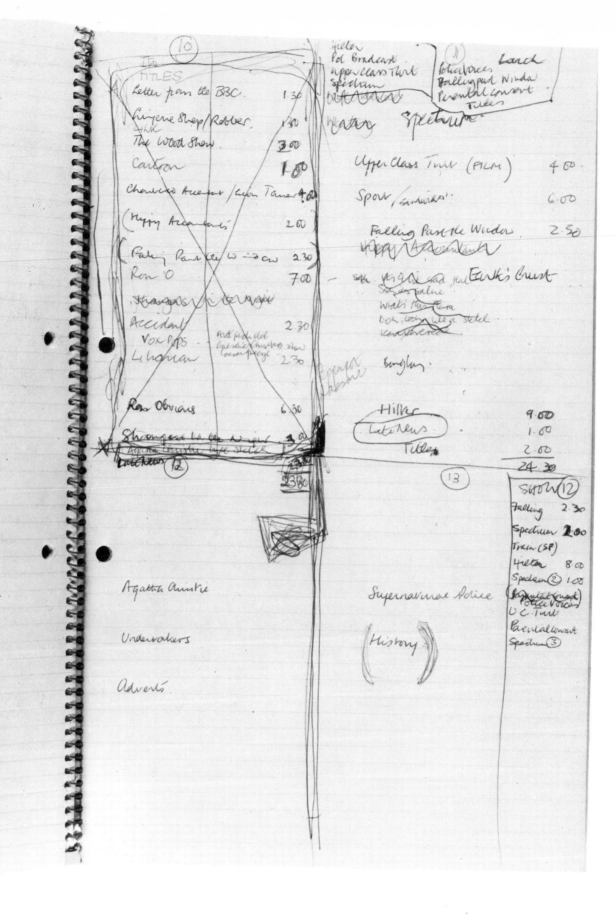

TITLES

Letter from the BBC.   1.30

Lingerie Shop/Robber.   1.30

The Wood Show   3.00

Cartoon   1.00

Chartered Accountant/Lion Tamer 4.00

("Happy Accountants"   2.00

Falling Past the W → 3 cw   2.30
Ron 'O   7.00

Strangers in the Night

Accident   2.30
Vox Pops
Librarian   2.30

Rem Obvious   6.30

Strangers in the Night   3.00
Late News   12

Agatha Christie

Undertakers

Adverts.

Hilton
Pol Broadcast
Upper Class Twit
Spectrum

Spectrum

Upper Class Twit (FILM)   4.00

Sport/   6.00

Falling Past the Window   2.30

Erik's Cr....

Bunglow.

Hilton   9.00
Late News   1.00
Titles   2.00
                    24.30

Police Voices   Lunch
Falling past Window
Parental Consent
Titles

13

Supernatural Police

(History)

SHOW 12
Falling   2.30
Spectrum   2.00
Train (SF)
Hilton   8.00
Spectrum ②   1.00
Police Voices
U C Twit
Parental consent
Spectrum ③

to the point of balance of the group. But there is no leader, and an absolute insistence on equality and unanimity in decision taking. John Cleese has sometimes been treated as the spokesman, but it is Cleese, as spokesman, who has called the group 'Democracy gone mad'.

The Pythons' mutual competitiveness is balanced by mutual respect. They were all measuring each other's writing and performing capabilities for more than half a decade before they recruited each other; they were not an artificial team brought together by a producer, but the synthesis of a whole series of mutually competing teams of script writers. The fact that they were also the performers heightened the creative tension, for there was no one but themselves to blame. Except, of course, the BBC, but we are coming to that.

The Pythons have created for themselves the hardest school of script-writing in the world: mutual respect is a condition that encourages ruthless mutual criticism. The technique evolved is known as the writing-meeting. For their television programmes, which had no determined structure beyond the running-time and the budget available, the team would work in its constituent elements – Cleese and Chapman, Palin and Jones, Idle alone, and Gilliam concentrating on his separate medium of animation. A writing-meeting, such as this early one in Terry Jones's house, brought the group together and each unit read/performed the material prepared. Eric Idle has said, 'It's the worst audience in the world. If you get big laughs there then the piece is in.' After arguments and changes, recorded in their notebooks, a running order would be painfully prepared (both Idle's and Palin's handwriting is on the page illustrated), a script typed and sent to the BBC.

This, the Python method, is still the primary source of the group's energy. Each member has to fight for his work and to defeat the creative rivalry of the others, and at times the arguments can be bitter. But when the method is working well it is not just a matter of having so much material brought to the meeting that all but the very best can be discarded; ideas from one unit are taken away and remoulded by another. The 'Ministry of Silly Walks' is a good example. It began somewhere in rejected material of Chapman's that included a number of government departments with silly names and functions. Later, stuck for an idea one morning, Palin and Jones developed Chapman's fragment into the 'Ministry of Silly Walks'. The material came back to the meeting, was worked over again and, when it came to the casting, Cleese was the obvious choice as the silly walker. And so a trade-mark was born.

The Python method was as important a factor in the success of the television series as the free-form stream of consciousness for which they became famous. Indeed, material written by them for a conventional

CARTOON INTRO - SPORTSVIEW DONE IN 4 CORNERS. SPORTSVIEW MUSIC

A BUSY STREET. OUT OF UNDERGROUND STATION COMES A CITY GENT.
"HISTORY OF SILLY WALKS" WELL DRESSED MAN WHO JUMPS IN A SITTING POSITION
THEN WALKS THREE PACES ... JUMPS AGAIN, WALKS THREE
PACES ... IN SHORT HE HAS A SILLY WALK.
FOLLOW HIM, AS HE BUYS PAPER .. GOES ALONG STREET, TURNS INTO
IMPOSING FACADE.
STIRRING MUSIC. C.U. PLACARD "MINISTRY OF SILLY WALKS".
CUT TO CORRIDOR, PEOPLE PASSING BY WITH SILLY WALKS ...
HE TURNS INTO OFFICE ...
GOES IN SITS DOWN, THERE IS A MAN SITTING THERE.

Good morning, sorry to keep you waiting, but my watch has become
sillier recently, and it ... takes me longer to get to work.
Now know what was it again.

Well Sir, I have a silly walk, and I would if possible like to
obtain a grant from the government to help silly walkers like
myself ... this silly walk ... develop it ...

I see, can I see your silly walk ..

Yes, certainly.
(He gets up, and does a few steps, lifting the bottom part
of his leg sharply every alternate).

That's it ... is it ?

Yes, that's it sir.

... Mr ... It's not particularly silly is it ?, ... I mean
the right leg isn't silly at all, and the left leg really does ... forward
well half turn every alternate step

But with government backing sir, I feel I could make it a lot more
silly

Mr. Stanford (He gets up) ... the real problem is one of money,
department has ... You see silly walk is no longer
getting the kind of support it need ... You see the
Defence, ... National Health, Housing, Education - silly walks. They're
all supposed to get the same. Last year the government spent less on
silly - walks than it did on ... Industrial Reorganisation

sketches-with-punchline format would have been just as strong, for everything must get past the collective criticism of six people who all know that they have the highest standards, and who do not agree amongst themselves what those highest standards are. The writing-meeting is not unique, any more than free-form comedy is original (Spike Milligan had shown the way with his television show *Q5*, which is why when they began they asked to work with Milligan's director, Ian MacNaughton), but the powerful forces inside the group made the furnace hotter and the material that finally emerged stronger. There was, however, one consequence of the Python method which made conflict with authorities and constraints inevitable. It first began to show itself in relation to the BBC and it was to be the source of all the Pythons' future disputes with authority. But also, it should be added, the source of their success.

This is not a book about the theory of comedy, and it would be self-defeating to write about the Pythons if it were, but it is clear that one of the ways to get a laugh is to surprise or shock. The surprise can be the portly gentleman slipping on a banana skin, or it can be the pompous idea turned on its head. Rude words, the common coin of ordinary speech, sound shocking when transmitted by the same medium that brings us Prince Charles's wedding, though it is impossible to conceive what threat such words contain. The Pythons were quick to exploit the humorous possibilities of bad language. Sex and comic violence (and much comedy is violence, either to people or ideas) are two obvious ways to shock an audience into laughter by breaking a convention. The most serious idea can be subverted by the absurd. (Which is why this is not a book about the theory of comedy.)

In the case of *Monty Python's Flying Circus* their first audience was themselves, and as Eric Idle has said, that was the worst audience in the world. Not only could it refuse to laugh, out of rivalry, jealousy and bad manners; it could turn round and write a parody of what you had written that would be accepted instead. It was a tough audience, made arrogant by a privileged education that – particularly at Cambridge – celebrated its verbal skills by making wounding comments, and it was an audience which, as it began to enjoy the liberating effects of fame and fortune, became increasingly hard to shock. A tough audience demands strong material and will accept no repetitions. There can only be one parrot sketch; after that all conversations between customers and shop assistants have to face that comparison. Even the Gumbies and the screaming, hard-hatted ladies known as Pepperpots, the Pythons' most distinctive familiars, have had a short life. The drive was always towards producing something that went further, that explored new areas for comedy, that brought the conventions down off the banana skin with a harder bang.

Of course it is unlikely that any Python would agree with this interpretation: all he would say is that they were trying to make people laugh. They had comic, not satiric, intentions, and even though, as John Cleese has said, they wanted to create a critical comedy that did something more than make jokes about the price of fish, laughs were what counted. But the comedy of shock (not, by any means, their only form of humour) has an inbuilt momentum. There was never at any time a conscious decision to challenge convention after convention, and tread on taboo after taboo, but it happened that way. One of the first to feel the Python foot was BBC Light Entertainment itself.

One of the ironies of *Monty Python*'s troubled relationship with the BBC is that only the BBC could have allowed its creation in the first place. *Monty Python's Flying Circus* is a vivid demonstration of Sir Hugh Carlton-Greene's principle, that 'Most of the best ideas must come from below, not from above.' The Pythons' view of the world, as producers and consumers of television comedy, was largely formed between 1960 and 1969, the period of Greene's service as Director-General of the BBC. In that time the BBC consolidated its position as a dominant cultural institution, but changed from a stuffy and snobbish organization following grudgingly in the wake of public opinion, to one which gently gave it a lead. This was the period when interviewers on current affairs programmes dropped their deferential attitude to those in power; when BBC television drama, both single plays like the social drama, *Cathy Come Home* and gritty police serials like *Z Cars*, presented viewers with a picture of British society that challenged comfortable assumptions among the middle class. The BBC never went *too* far, but it suggested that there were alternative views say, in the case of *That Was the Week That Was*, to the idea that politicians were gods, or in the case of *Till Death Us Do Part*, to the idea that bigotry did not exist. Greene introduced a period of creativity in the BBC and encouraged that creativity by leaving it alone:

No correspondent could do his work if he had an editor constantly breathing down his neck. And the same is true of producers. Nothing could be achieved by censorship or coercion, either from within the Corporation or from the outside – nothing, that is, except the frustration of creative people who achieve their best work by the conscious stimulation of their positive ideas.

Although Greene retired as Director-General of the BBC in April 1969, the Pythons were beneficiaries of his policies. They had more or less invented themselves as a group, and they were not even asked to produce a pilot programme for a comedy show for which they had no title and few fixed ideas. They were able to have the producer of their choice, Ian MacNaughton, and they dealt with no one but him. As far as MacNaughton's superiors were concerned, responsibility for the programme was his, and they did not ask to see scripts or preview programmes. They watched the programme at home, when it was transmitted, and if there were complaints, from inside or outside the Corporation, they were dealt with after, and not before, the creative decisions were made.

None of the Pythons can recall any difficulty over their first series, although they knew that the Head of Comedy's superior, the Head of Light Entertainment, Tom Sloan, could not understand the programme and disliked it intensely. Ironically, in the light of future events, the Pythons themselves practised a small piece of self-censorship when they cut a Gilliam cartoon of a telephone engineer working on a telegraph pole – which turns out to be one of the three crosses of Calvary.

The BBC made *Python* possible but the Pythons had chosen a bad time to evolve a form of comedy which depends on pushing ideas beyond their conventionally accepted limit. Just as the Pythons' creative confidence began to expand, the BBC's began to contract.

It is the proud claim of the BBC that for the Corporation, censorship does not exist. Technically that is true. Under Section 1(3) (b) of the Obscene Publications Act, 1959, broadcasting is specifically excluded. Nor is the BBC covered by the Theatres Act, 1968, and the form of censorship practised by the British Board of Film Censors has absolutely no application when a film is shown on television. The BBC is even protected from older legislation against causing an offence in a public place, because television and radio sets are kept in private places. In the view of the office of the Director of Public Prosecutions it would be quite impossible to apply to the BBC the law forbidding conspiracies to corrupt public morals or outrage public decency, firstly because very large numbers of people would have to demonstrate that they were outraged and secondly because it would be difficult to show that the

BBC is a conspiracy. The BBC is significantly freer than commercial television which, under the 1954 Television Act which established it, may not 'offend against good taste or decency'. Theoretically the BBC is completely free from government interference, unless the Home Secretary formally requires it to do something – and no Home Secretary has ever used this power.

The truth is somewhat different. The BBC is a major public institution, and like all public institutions it is subject to intense pressures from interested parties. Since the BBC is one of the country's principal means of communicating ideas, images and values, there are few interested parties who are not interested in the BBC. The parties with the most interest are political parties, and it is a measure of the BBC's success that it manages at times to offend Left, Right and Centre. Politicians are reluctant, when in office, to be seen to be manipulating the BBC, for out of office the same manipulations might be used against them, but they do have one crude instrument that makes sure that the BBC does not go too far – the level of the licence fee. The cost of a television licence (radio is free) is set by the government and administered by the Post Office, and it is the only form of revenue the BBC has, apart from what it earns by selling programmes abroad and other recycling operations. During the 1960s the steady expansion of television ownership and the introduction of colour television meant that the BBC was reasonably free from economic pressure. But by the beginning of the 1970s that expansion was over. As faster inflation began to set in the BBC's costs also began to rise more rapidly, while it was left with an inadequate revenue from a licence fee that the government was reluctant to increase because that would further contribute to the rise in the cost of living. In spite of BBC television being the cheapest service in Europe, a rise in the licence fee is always politically unpopular, and this factor in itself has been a means of keeping the BBC on a short rein, for if the BBC 'behaves itself' in the view of politicians, then an increase in the licence fee is grudgingly conceded, or the BBC is allowed to extend its borrowing. But the increase has never been enough for the BBC to regain financial independence. And if the BBC does not behave itself, well . . .

The politicians' judgment of the BBC's behaviour is formed first of all by the way its programmes conform to their own images of themselves, and throughout the sixties the BBC showed that it was quite capable of taking an irreverent line. But politicians are in turn subject to intense pressure from interested parties; and the irreverent and liberalizing attitudes of some BBC programmes offended not only politicians, but pressure groups among their constituents. The most celebrated of these is Mrs Mary Whitehouse and the National Viewers' and Listeners' Association. Mrs Whitehouse, a middle-aged school-teacher then living in Shropshire, became concerned about the influence of broadcasting on public morality in the early 1960s. A committed Christian and a former supporter of Moral Rearmament, she was worried by the secular attitude in schools towards the family and in particular by the morally neutral approach to sex education. She attributed a great deal of the changed moral attitudes among young people to the changed moral attitudes portrayed on television.

Mrs Whitehouse was not alone in her beliefs, for when she and Mrs Norah Buckland, with virtually no organization, decided to hold a meeting at Birmingham Town Hall on 5 May 1964, there was no difficulty in filling the hall to capacity. The simplicity of her message was summed up in the original title of her campaign, Clean Up TV, but it was plain that for it to be effective as a pressure group a more subtle and positive approach was necessary. On 16 March 1965 the National Viewers' and Listeners' Association was launched, with Mrs Whitehouse as Secretary, and this has been her power-base ever since. The precise number of her supporters is vague – in 1975 31,000 supporters were claimed – but Mrs Whitehouse has become a national figure of importance. She is partially the creation of the media she criticizes, but it is clear that she speaks for a section of the community that deplores many of the changes that have taken place in British society. One of the turning points in her career was the National Viewers' and Listeners' Association convention in May 1967, at which the support of Malcolm Muggeridge was crucial, and it was Muggeridge who in 1969 first suggested to her a 'Festival of Light'. The Nationwide Festival of Light which grew out of that suggestion, and which had its first rally in Trafalgar Square in 1971, was not organized directly by Mrs Whitehouse, but the same attitudes prevail in both organizations. 1971 was a year of particular tension between would-be liberators and would-be defenders of decency. It was the year of Lord Longford's investigation into pornography (in which Mrs Whitehouse participated) and it was the year in which the editors of the underground magazine Oz were successfully prosecuted under the Obscene Publications Act for their 'School Kids' issue. When the prison sentences passed on the Oz editors were quashed on appeal in January 1972, Mrs Whitehouse launched a 'Nationwide Petition for Public Decency', a plea for more than just a clean-up of television. Both the Viewers' and Listeners' Association and the Festival of Light collected the 1,350,000 signatures on the petition presented to the then Prime Minister, Mr Heath, in April 1973.

The National Viewers' and Listeners' Association, or National VALA as Mrs Whitehouse likes to call it, playing on the acronym, is only one of the many ways in which public opinion is brought to bear on the BBC. Mrs Whitehouse has tried to prosecute the BBC, and the veteran anti-pornography campaigner, Raymond

Blackburn, took out a writ against the BBC in 1975 following reports of plans for a television film about pornographers by the Open University. The Festival of Light has its own voice. Politicians have their private channels, and there is the simple direct method of individuals writing to the BBC, a practice which National VALA encourages. The press, ignoring the beam in its own eye, is quick to attack any hint of bias. The BBC has its own 'public conscience' in the shape of its Chairman and Board of Governors, distinguished and worthy people in public life who are appointed by the government to oversee the activities of the Director-General and the Board of Management. Sir Hugh Carlton-Greene, like Lord Reith before the war, was such a strong Director-General that the BBC Governors were relatively powerless, but as we have seen, the style of the BBC under Greene's leadership had given offence to a number of pressure groups and a number of politicians. Among them was Britain's Labour Prime Minister from 1964 to 1970, Harold Wilson.

In 1967 Harold Wilson had an opportunity to appoint a new Chairman for the BBC Board of Governors. He chose as his man a former Conservative politician, Lord Hill of Luton, who had been famous as the 'Radio Doctor' in the 1940s and notorious as the leader of the British Medical Association's campaign against the introduction of the National Health Service. It was not Hill's political past, however, that made his appointment astonishing, but his immediately previous job. Since 1963 he had been Chairman of the Independent Television Authority (now the IBA), which supervises the activities of the commercial television companies. There was no love lost between the BBC and independent television, and it was an unpleasant shock for the higher management to learn who their new Chairman was. Not only that, Hill had a reputation as an interventionist chairman. As he proudly records in his memoirs, it was he who introduced a system at the ITA for vetting feature programmes before they went out.

Since no one would admit it, even if it were true, it is impossible to state categorically that Harold Wilson appointed Lord Hill to punish the BBC for its real or imagined slights on him. Hill states that he was not asked 'to do a hatchet job on the BBC' but it is clear that Wilson knew the characteristics of the man he was appointing, and one of those characteristics was to be an active Chairman, with consequent implications for the role of Greene. Members of the National Viewers' and Listeners' Association had their own interpretation. One of them wrote to Mrs Whitehouse that Lord Hill's appointment was a 'miracle', and, since Lord Hill was soon courteously receiving a delegation from National VALA, where Greene had always refused, Mrs Whitehouse had every reason to be pleased by the appointment. 'With Lord Hill at the BBC,' she wrote, 'sharper eyes were being focussed on the scripts.'

The change in the creative atmosphere following Lord Hill's appointment at the BBC took place very slowly, while he established his position and got the backing of new and firmer-fibred members of the Board of Governors. Even after Greene's early retirement in 1969 the ideas continued to flow from the bottom to the top.

Down at the bottom the Pythons were busy writing, rehearsing, filming and recording their first series. Their arguments with the BBC were over the more usual matters that worry artistes: publicity and transmission times. They were furious when the publicity department, without any consultation with them, described the new show as 'satirical', a word they would have given anything to avoid, and 'nutty, zany and oddball' were not exactly completely different either. Their persistent complaint, however, was that they were unable to build up an audience (and so prove their worth), because the show never went out at the same time of night, and indeed sometimes did not go out at all. On 5 November 1969 they were replaced by Christopher Isherwood talking to Derek Hart; on 12 November viewers expecting to see *Monty Python* found the Duke of Edinburgh instead.

In spite of what they regarded as the wilful negligence of the programme planners, the Pythons managed to increase their average audience from one-and-a-half to three million, and once, when by some accident the show was transmitted as early as 9.45 p.m., the viewing figures reached four-and-a-half. The Python cult was mysterious to many, but delightful to a few. Unfortunately the higher echelons of the BBC appeared to be among the many. Terry Gilliam's animations gave the show a distinctive style, and the free association of the cartoon links fed back into the presentation of the rest of the script. Unlike the others, Gilliam had a certain autonomy over his contributions. The others could not control his work through writing-meetings, because his expositions chiefly consisted of grunts, gestures and explosions, so he was usually given in-cues and out-cues and freedom to go where he liked in between. The comic violence traditional in animated cartoons worked its way out into the other performances. The violence was partly accidental: Gilliam freely admits that he knew almost nothing about animation when he started, and the quick, sharp movement is much easier to use than slow and subtle curves. The Python foot comes crashing down because Gilliam did not know any other way to get it there. But there was also an inherent savagery in the sketches, particularly those written by Cleese and Chapman, typified by a rejected title for the programme, *Owl Stretching Time*.

The first series of *Monty Python* ended on 11 January 1970 and the BBC judged it successful enough to commission another, for which recording began in June that year. The budget was increased from the parsimonious £3,500 per show to £4,500 and the Pythons

MONTY PYTHON'S FLYING CIRCUS

Sex and Violence

Designer: Christopher Thompson

Producer: John Howard Davies and Ian McNaughton

Sunday, 12th October 1969, 11.10-11.35 pm, BBC 1

1. <u>Size of audience</u> (based on results of the Survey of Listening and Viewing).

It is estimated that the audience for this broadcast was 2.9% of the United Kingdom population. Programmes on BBC 2 and ITV at the time were seen by 0.5% and 14.8% (averages).

2. <u>Reaction of audience</u> (based on questionnaires completed by a sample of the audience. This sample, 74 in number, is the 3% of the BBC 1 Viewing Panel who saw all or most of the broadcast).

The reactions of this small sample of the audience were distributed as follows:

A+	A	B	C	C-
%	%	%	%	%
12	37	27	5	19

giving a REACTION INDEX of 55. The first programme in the series gained a figure of 45. By way of comparison, The World of Beachcomber began in January last year with a figure of . . . . average . . . that first BBC 2 series

got what they had missed in the first series, an earlier and regular starting time, just after ten o'clock on Tuesdays. This was late enough, but the real trouble was that this was the time when the BBC regions left the network to show their own programmes, so only London and the Northern Region saw *Python*, and even then the series was interrupted by *The Horse of the Year Show*. The Pythons worked off some of their anger in sketches about programme planners, and more positively by writing a letter of protest to the Controller of BBC1, Paul Fox. The series was being rehearsed and recorded as it went out, and during rehearsals they were pleased to receive a placatory visit from Huw Wheldon, BBC Television's Managing Director, who promised that the *Radio Times* would after all give the show some publicity during its run. He also announced that he had arranged a meeting for them with Paul Fox. Collectively the Pythons can be an intimidating sight, and their numbers have given them the edge in several disputes. The following week they massed in Paul Fox's office (there was hardly room for them all to sit down) to hear his explanation of the reasons for the low budget, the loss of an assistant and the dreadful programme placing. In fact there

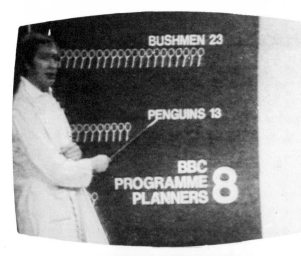

was little that could be done, and Fox promised that there would be repeats at a better time, but the Pythons were beginning to flex their muscles and argue with the BBC.

They also had something up their sleeve. Now fully confident of their creative power, in the last show of Series II, number 13, they rounded things off with a bang by entering the controversial question of the comedy of death – and threw in cannibalism for good measure.

The writers of the notorious 'Undertakers' sketch

compared with primitive human sub groups such as the Bush men of the Kalahari but better than BBC Programme planners (HE REFERS TO GRAPH DECORATED WITH LITTLE RACQUETS WHICH SHOWS BUSHMEN WITH 23 PENGUINS WITH 13 AND BBC PRO. PLANNERS WITH 8) The BBC Programme Planners surprisingly high total here can be explained away as being within the ordinary limits of statistical error. One particularly dim programme planner can cock the whole thing up.

(CUT TO FILM. TENNIS PLAYER IN CHANGING ROOM TAKING OFF GYM SHOES. IN BACKGROUND TWO OTHER PLAYERS DISCUSS SHOTS. CAPTION. DR LEWIS HOAD)

H.
Hallo.

(CAPTION. READER IN FOREHAND PASSING SHOTS
        FOREST HILLS UNIV).

(CUT BACK TO HOAD)

H.
These I.Q. tests were thought to contain an unfair cultural bias against the penguins. For example they did not take into account the penguins poor educational system. To devise fairer tests a team of our researchers spent 18 months in Antarctica living like penguins and subsequently dying like penguins, only quicker, showing that the penguin is a clever little sod in his own environment.

(CUT BACK TO DROBNY IN STUDIO)

S.
Therefore we devised tests to be given to the penguins in the fourth set. I do beg your pardon. In their own environment. (SHOUT OF 'LET') Sssssh!

(CUT TO FILM OF A SCIENTIST WITH A COUPLE OF ASSISTANTS SURROUNDING A KNOT OF PENGUINS IN A PENGUIN POOL)

PROFESSOR
(AGAIN IN TENNIS CLOTHES BUT WITH EINSTEIN HAIR AND GLASSES) What is the next number in this sequence two four six (PENGUIN HONKS) Did he say eight?

(WE SEE USUAL UMPIRE SITTING IN HIGH CHAIR NEARBY)

S. SPEAKING
The environmental barrier had been removed but we'd hit another. The penguins could not speak English and were therefore unable to give answers.

STUDIO AGAIN

S. SPEAKING
This problem was removed in the next series of experiments by asking the same questions to the penguins and to a random group of non English-speaking humans in the same conditions.

U:
Hallo!

MAN:
Good morning.

U:
What can I do you for squire?

MAN:
Well I wonder if you can help me...my mother
has just died and I'm not quite sure what to do.

U:
Oh well we can help you. We deal with stiffs.

MAN:
Stiffs?

U:
Yeah, there's three things we can do with your
mum. We can bury her, burn her or dump her.

MAN:
Dump her?

U:
Dump her in the Thames.

MAN:
What?

U:
Oh did you like her?

MAN:
Yes.

U:
Oh well we won't dump her then. Well what do
you think. A burner or a buryer.

MAN:
Well which do you recommend.

U:
Well, they're both nasty... Well with a burner,
we stuff her in the fire, and she goes up in
smoke, bit of a shock if she's not quite dead,
but quick, and then we give you a box of ashes,
which you can pretend are hers.

MAN:
Oh.

U:
Or if you don't want to fry her, we can bury
her and then she'll get eaten up by maggots and
weevils, which isn't so hot if, as I said,
she's not quite dead.

MAN:
I see. Well err I'm not very sure she's
definitely dead.

U:
Where is she?

MAN:
She's in this sack.

U:
Let's have a look (LOOKS) Oh! She looks quite
young.

MAN:
Yes she was.

U:
Fred!

were Chapman and Cleese. Graham Chapman remembers the afternoon they wrote it as one of the
funniest of his life; John Cleese has said, 'If you could
have seen us writing it, it was not two calculating
members of the IRA planning to destroy the world, but
two young men holding their sides and shaking with
laughter.' The sketch was brought to a writing-
meeting in the garden of Terry Jones's house in Cam-
berwell. Terry Gilliam collapsed with laughter and
remained hysterical for the rest of the day, but Idle,
Palin and Jones were more shocked. Terry Jones, who
had elderly parents, remembers being called away to
the phone and thinking that they couldn't put this one
out. 'But then, why not? We think it's funny.' So in
accordance with the Python method the sketch was
included, a script typed and sent to the BBC.

As producer, Ian MacNaughton felt less sure and he
took the precaution of 'referring' the script upwards.
'Reference upwards' is the BBC's system of self-
censorship. If a producer is unsure of his ground, he
seeks senior advice, and the matter can go as high as
the Director-General if a difficult decision has to be
made. In this case the Head of Comedy, Michael Mills,
read the script and said that it was all right, provided
that the audience was shown to register its disap-
proval by taking over the set. (In fact a truly disapprov-
ing reaction would have been a shocked silence – Eric
Idle remembers the sharp intakes of breath when he
performed the sketch on their Canadian stage tour.)

For reasons of confusion and fire precautions the audience protests were not made absolutely clear in the recording, and the script was as meaty as it had been written. On the night of transmission the Pythons added insult to injury by repeating the sketch at the start of a cheeky appearance on BBC2's discussion programme, *Late Night Line-Up*. (The sketch was *Line-Up*'s choice.)

The 'Undertakers' sketch was transmitted on 22 December 1970; the following day the senior management of BBC Television met at a controllers' meeting. The Pythons were already unpopular for providing Stanley Reynolds with material for an article in *The Times* which discussed at length 'the sort of opposition within the BBC which logically should have killed off the comedy series'. The minutes of the meeting show how uncomfortable the management felt about the monster it had fostered.

comme......... by .... Sims (H.C.F......)

"Monty Python's Flying Circus" (BBC-1)

Aubrey Singer (H.F.G.Tel.) said that he had found parts of this edition disgusting. C.BBC-1 said the programme was continually going over the edge of what was acceptable; this edition had contained two really awful sketches; the death sequence had been in appalling taste, while the treatment of the national anthem had simply not been amusing. Bill Cotton (H.L.E.G.Tel.) did not think that the situation had been helped by the further appearance of the programme team in "Line-Up", about which the producer had never told him.

- 11 -   23 December 1970

356.   M.D.Tel. said it must be recognised that in the past   356
Cont.   the programme had contained dazzle and produced some
            very good things; but this edition had been quite
            certainly over the edge, and the producer Ian
            McNaughton, had failed to refer it when he should
            have done so. Stephen Hearst (H.A.F.Tel.) was
            critical of the fact that the values of the programme
            were so nihilistic and cruel. Desmond Wilcox
            (Editor, "Man Alive") asked what was wrong with cruel
            humour, but Bob Reid (H.S.F.Tel.) felt the team
            seemed often to wallow in the sadism of their humour.
            C.BBC-2 thought they also shied away from responsibility.
            D.P.Tel. said the episode had been a sad end for the
            series.

            Bill Cotton (H.L.E.G.Tel.) said it would be very sad
            if the BBC lost the programme, currently the team
            seemed to have some sort of death wish; he hoped that
            a new series could be brought back in 1972.

            "International Golf: The Best 18" (BBC-2)

Glossary: HFGTel = Head of Features Group, Television, Aubrey Singer
             CBBC-1 = Programme Controller, BBC1, Paul Fox
             HLEGTel = Head of Light Entertainment Group, Television, Bill Cotton
             MDTel = Managing Director, BBC Television, Huw Wheldon
             HAFTel = Head of Arts Features, Television, Stephen Hearst
             HSFTel = Head of Science Features, Television, Bob Reid
             CBBC-2 = Director of Programmes, Television, David Attenborough

The management then turned to discussing how much they had enjoyed a programme about golf.

The Pythons *were* brought back, for a third series, which started recordings in December 1971 but did not go out until the autumn of 1972. As Stanley Reynolds commented in *The Times*, 'it is hard to believe that BBC bosses can be so unaware of so successful a product', and indeed they were not. Within the BBC the Pythons' position was strengthened by winning the Silver Rose at the Montreux Festival in 1971, and the Pythons were well launched into other enterprises like books, records and a feature film. But the BBC was decidedly wary. The last show of the second series has never been repeated by the BBC, and in some BBC recordings the 'Undertakers' sketch has disappeared. Nor has the show been sold abroad, although the Pythons suspect that this may be due to the programme's levity towards the royal family as much as death. For Series III the scripts had to be read in advance by the management and all the recordings were previewed. The Pythons had in part provoked this, but throughout the BBC the system of a rare 'reference upwards' was being reversed into a general monitoring downwards.

Back at the top, in his office in Broadcasting House, Lord Hill had been taking steps to keep the managers themselves under firmer control, for the content and style of plays and political reporting were giving cause for concern. He stoutly resisted Mrs Whitehouse's demands for the creation of a broadcasting council, but fended off outside pressure by creating controls and watchdogs of his own, an Advisory Group on the Social Effects of Television, and the Broadcasting Complaints Commission, which delivered its first verdicts in July 1972. In late 1971 he decided that it was time to open discussions with the senior staff about the general area of 'taste and sex'. He wrote in his diary for 21 October:

> I hope it will lead to a voluntary decision by the senior executives themselves to take discreet steps and so avoid a breach between the Governors and our creative staff. This may sound like timidity but I have learned from experience that ideas which our senior staff people have formed or believe that they themselves have formed are more likely to be effective than *obiter dicta* from above.

2. Reaction Profile (based on 199 questionnaires completed by 21% of the Viewing Panel).

Viewers were asked to rate the broadcast on four dimensions defined by pairs of adjectives or descriptive phrases. Their selection of one of five scale positions between each pair resulted in the following reaction profile:

	%	%	%	%	%	
Very vulgar	9	31	38	9	13	Completely clean
Very funny	37	24	13	10	16	Thoroughly unfunny
Very sophisticated	21	23	27	13	16	Completely corny
Artists excellent	46	24	16	4	10	Poor

3. There were strong contrasts in the sample's response, although more viewers were entertained than not.

4. At one extreme, a good many reporting viewers agreed that this edition was 'funny all the way through', some describing it as 'the best to date' and the show as one of the best on TV. A sizeable minority, however, found nothing amusing in it at all, quite often describing it in terms such as 'utter rot', 'below the normal level of intelligence', 'puerile nonsense'. The fact that it was not 'completely clean' did not necessarily affect viewers' response, but some complained that it was rather too 'crude in places' and at the lowest level there were objections that it was 'disgusting'. Among moderately pleased viewers, some remarked that this particular edition was not as amusing as usual or went rather too far, for example in the 'Salad Days' item. Objections to this item at various levels in the sample ranged from complaints that it was rather too 'horrific', 'sick' and 'gory', to protests that it was 'repulsive', distasteful' and 'unnecessary'. Generally speaking, however, the sketches seemed to have been very much enjoyed by rather more than half the sample and the animations by nearly as many, and disliked to varying degrees by one in five (in the first case) and one in four (in the second).

5. Opinions of the artists coincided with feelings abo᠎   how as a whole ('shoot the lot! was the advice of one viewer, fo᠎   ᠎ose who did not ᠎᠎᠎᠎ the show seemed to a᠎᠎᠎᠎ ᠎᠎

The comment is a model of manipulative Establishment thinking. The censored are to be led to believe that they are censoring themselves (though it is difficult to imagine that the senior staff of the BBC would be fooled into believing that these were ideas 'they themselves had formed'). And self-censorship is infinitely preferable to any formal rules or regulations whose existence could lead to their being challenged.

Lord Hill's discussions with his management, who included some of the angry commentators on the 'Undertakers' sketch, continued into 1972. It was a difficult time for the BBC. There had been a major row over the decision to transmit *The Question of Ulster – an Enquiry into the Future* which the then Home Secretary, Reginald Maudling, had publicly urged the BBC not to broadcast, and the tension in Northern Ireland caused continual problems over reporting the bloody events there. In June 1971 a sour programme about the effect of losing power on members of the former Labour Government, *Yesterday's Men*, risked destroying the tolerance of both Labour and Conservative politicians towards the BBC. (Which in itself reveals the true attitude of politicians to the Corporation.)

At the beginning of 1972 Lord Hill received a deputation from the Festival of Light and, in order to get a clearer idea of their views, he asked for a formal paper, which arrived three months later. Hill comments: 'Some points in the Festival's document were regarded as fair, indeed they had often been expressed in board meetings. For example, it was said that nowadays some creative artists wanted to use artistic freedom to go to lengths which were indefensible for broadcasting.'

Against this background of mounting pressure on the BBC and a changed attitude within it, the Pythons were completing the recording of Series III. By the spring of 1972, after two years of more or less continuous production of Python material, there was considerable tension within the group, and arguments were not being settled as amicably as before. Cleese had declared that he wanted to leave at the end of the second series but was persuaded to stay on, although in his opinion the search for new ideas was making them thrash about, exploiting the strange and violent rather than the funny. The BBC's Audience Research Unit, which was now monitoring 'questions of sex and taste' as well as entertainment, has produced evidence that some of the audience for Series III thought so too. The Python television style, however, had been perfected, and the idea of what a comedy series was supposed to be completely changed. In three years they had moved from minority cult to acknowledged mastery of the School of British nonsense. The term 'pythonesque' was firmly established in the language.

On 25 May 1972 the Pythons were surprised to see both the Head of the Light Entertainment Group, Bill Cotton, and the Head of Comedy, Duncan Wood, at their last recording for the series. Their presence was

In his latest film Peckinpah has moved into the calmer and more lyrical waters of Julian Slade's Salad Days.

CUT TO:

FILM OF SALAD DAYS AS FROM HALFWAY DOWN PAGE TWO.

SUPERIMPOSE

SALAD DAYS (1971) DIRECTOR SAM PECKINPAH

(THE BOYS AND GIRLS CEASE FROLICKING AND SINGING. MICHAEL PALIN ENTERS AS LIONEL, HOLDING A TENNIS RACKET)

L:
Hallo everybody.

ALL:
Hallo Lionel.

L:
What a simply super day.

ALL:
Gosh yes.

BEULAH:
Yes it's so, well, you know, sunny I mean.

L:
Yes isn't it? I say anyone for tennis?

JULIAN:
Oh super!

CHARLES:
What fun.

JULIAN:
Hey Lionel catch.

(HE THROWS THE TENNIS BALL TO LIONEL. IT HITS LIONEL ON THE HEAD. LIONEL CLAPS ONE HAND TO HIS FOREHEAD. HE ROARS IN PAIN AS BLOOD SEEPS THROUGH HIS FINGERS.)

LIONEL:
Oh golly!

(HE TOSSES HIS RACKET OUT OF FRAME AND WE HEAR A HIDEOUS SCREAM. CAMERA PANS SLIGHTLY TO PICK UP PRETTY GIRL IN SUMMER FROCK WITH THE HANDLE OF THE RACKET EMBEDDED IN HER STOMACH, BLOOD IS POURING OUT DOWN HER DRESS)

GIRL:
(IN PAIN) Oh gosh!

(SPITTING BLOOD OUT OF HER MOUTH SHE COLLAPSES ONTO THE FLOOR, CLUTCHING AT CHARLES' ARM. THE ARM COMES OFF. BUCKETS OF BLOOD BURST OUT OF THE SHOULDER DRENCHING THE GIRL AND ANYONE ELSE IN THE AREA)

CHARLES:
Sorry, Wendy!

(HE STAGGERS BACKWARDS AGAINST THE PIANO. THE PIANO LID DROPS, SEVERING THE PIANIST'S HANDS. PIANIST SCREAMS. HE STANDS, BLOOD SPURTING FROM HIS HANDS OVER PIANO MUSIC. PIANO IS COLLAPSING IN SLOW MOTION. SHOT FROM SEVERAL ANGLES SIMULTANEOUSLY AS PER ZABRISKY POINT A LA END OF FRENCH RUBBISH DUMP FILM.

INTERCUT. TERRIFIED FACES OF GIRLS SCREAMING IN SLOW MOTION. THE PIANO EVENTUALLY CRUSHES THEM TO DEATH... ENORMOUS POOL OF BLOOD IMMEDIATELY SWELLS UP FROM BENEATH PIANO WHERE THE GIRLS ARE. WE SEE JULIAN STAGGER ACROSS THE FRAME WITH THE PIANO KEYBOARD THROUGH HIS STOMACH. AS HE TURNS THE END OF THE KEYBOARD KNOCKS OFF THE HEAD OF A TERRIFIED GIRL WHO IS SITTING ON THE GRASS NEARBY. A VOLCANIC QUANTITY (REALLY VAST)

'Allo. 'Allo. Cor what a bit of stuff. I'd
like to get my plates of meat around those
milkers. (HE POUNCES UPON LADY 2 THROWS HER
SKIRTS OVER HER HEAD AND PUSHES HER OVER THE
BACK OF THE SOFA)

LADY 1:
Ah, vicar, how perfectly delightful to see you.
I hope you're settling down in your new parish.
(THE VICAR HAS DISAPPEARED) How do you find the
Vicarage? (CLOTHES APPEAR FROM OVER BACK OF
COUCH) Poor Rev. Wheeler used to find it so
damp in the winter, I believe.

(VICAR STANDS UP FROM BEHIND SOFA, HIS SHIRT
OPEN AND HIS HAIR AWRY. HE REACHES OVER AND
PUTS HIS HAND DOWN LADY 1'S FRONT)

VIC:
I like tits!

LADY 1:
Oh Vicar! Vicar!

(VICAR SUDDENLY PULLS BACK AND LOOKS AROUND HIM
AS IF IN THE HORROR OF DAWNING REALISATION)

VICAR:
Oh dear! I do beg your pardon...How simply
awful...My first day in my new parish...
dreadful...I completely lost my head...

LADY 1:
(READJUSTING HER DRESS) Yes well, never mind.
Chivers! Send Mary in with a new gown.

(LADY 2 STRUGGLES TO HER FEET FROM BEHIND COUCH,
COMPLETELY DESHABILLE HER OWN GOWN COMPLETELY
RIPPED OPEN.)

VICAR:
(TO LADY 2) Oh let me help you... I do beg your
pardon.

LADY 1:
Well, as I was saying how do you find the new
vicarage?

(THEY TAKE THEIR SEATS ON THE COUCH)

VICAR:
Oh find...yes indeed...yes certainly...I find
the grounds delightful and the servants
attentive, particularly that scullery maid with
the long eyelashes and the bigoooh! When she
bends over to scrub the floor oooh. Those great
big bristols hang down...oooooh!

(HE THROWS HIMSELF ON THE HOSTESS ACROSS THE
TEA TABLE, KNOCKING IT OVER AND THEY DISAPPEAR
OVER THE BACK OF THE HOSTESSES CHAIR.
GRUNTS ETC.)

(ENTER DICKIE APPLAUDING. ALSO, WE HEAR
AUDIENCE APPLAUSE)

VICAR:
Well there we are, another year has been too
soon alas ended, and I think none more than
myself can be happier at this time than I...
am.

(THE VICAR AND LADY 1 ARE STILL AT IT ON THE
FLOOR. THE BUTLER, LADY 2 AND THE SWISS
MOUNTAINEER STAND IN A LINE AT THE BACK,

ominous, and the Pythons heard in the BBC Club
afterwards that Cotton and Wood were not happy
about the last two shows they had recorded, not
happy at all. But it was not a problem over whether the
shows were funny. Michael Palin noted in his diary:
'This is the first time they have ever suggested any
censorship, in what has been a quite outspoken
series.' How outspoken it would be allowed to be
when it was transmitted in the autumn was now in
doubt. Ian MacNaughton, as producer, found himself
caught between the pressure of the Pythons, to whom
he felt a certain loyalty, and the BBC, for whom he was
working on a short-term contract.

The position was made more complicated by the fact
that MacNaughton and the Pythons were going to
Germany, where they were to make a special show
(their second) for Bavarian television. The BBC's initial
proposal was that the last two shows in the new series,
numbers 12 and 13, should be cannibalized into a
single thirty-minute episode, something the Pythons
would not agree to. MacNaughton asked for details of
the objectionable items to be put in writing and sent to
him in Germany. This letter became known as 'The
Thirty-Two Points of Worry', for it proposed a number
of cuts, varying in length from whole sketches to
single words. Sadly, no copy of this letter seems to
have survived outside the BBC, but among the items
listed were a wine taster offering only wee-wee; upper-
class twits in a city bar asking for revolting cocktails
such as mallard fizz; most of a sketch about a dirty
vicar; and a scene at the Café Royal where Oscar Wilde
and Co. compete in insulting the Prince of Wales.
More seems to have been read into the material by the
management than was intended: a glass of red wine
was taken to be menstrual blood, and there were complaints about 'the big penis that comes through the
door' – in fact, a severed arm. There was also objection
to the words, 'and masturbation'.

Ian MacNaughton's first attempt to deflect the cuts was met with a much curter letter ordering that the changes be made, and while he prevaricated from Germany further cuts were demanded. At the insistence of the Pythons, MacNaughton arranged a meeting with the Head of Comedy, Duncan Wood. The first programmes of the new series had already been transmitted when on 27 October 1972 all six Pythons and MacNaughton crowded into Wood's office. Their main objection was to the volume of the cuts, which seemed ridiculous in a show going out after ten o'clock at night, but Terry Jones made a spirited defence of masturbation. 'What's wrong with masturbation?' he is reported to have exploded. 'I masturbate, you masturbate . . .' The Head of Comedy made no reply to this assertion. The Pythons' real difficulty was in discovering why censorship was being tightened. Wood spoke of 'pressures from outside', but from whom these came or what form they took was not revealed.

The implication was that the pressure was coming from the top (literally so, since senior executives work on the seventh floor of the Television Centre), which could only mean the Controller of BBC1, Paul Fox. Indeed, one of the cuts demanded was a piece of animation using a photograph of Fox, but it turned out that Fox had not seen the offending programmes. Accordingly, a viewing was agreed to, with the strange proviso that MacNaughton should not be present when the Controller watched the shows. The result was a moral victory for the Pythons and for the BBC, for Paul Fox decided that only three minor changes were necessary. His comment on the 'Prince of Wales' sketch was, 'I don't much like "a dose of clap"; but who does?' It was too late to save 'and masturbation', however, for the 'All England Summarize Proust Competition' in show five had already been transmitted, with Graham Chapman listing his hobbies as 'golf, strangling animals—' and silence. Only lip readers could know his unmentionable vice.

The dispute over whether you can use the word 'masturbation' for comic effect in a Summarize Proust Competition summarizes most of the arguments between the Pythons and the BBC. In the fourth series, recorded in 1974 without Cleese, the word 'condom' did not even get to the recording stage, and there was constant bargaining over the amount of coarse language they could use. If they gave up four 'shits' they could have one 'bugger', and so forth. In fact the terms under which the BBC could edit material after it had been accepted were strictly controlled by contract, and the Pythons never found it necessary to go to arbitration. That is because six angry, arrogant Pythons were usually a match for the BBC, and they had always chosen to fight their own battles over editing as well as publicity and programming, rather than go through their agents. They acknowledged the license the BBC had given them, but by 1974 the atmosphere was radically changed.

During yet another row over words in the fourth series the Pythons were told that they must accept the BBC's view: censorship was a fact. While the Pythons wanted to go further – not so much in terms of rough language, which was becoming a convention in itself, and so must be broken, but into new areas of comedy – the BBC felt it necessary to rein in, and was much more ready to admit to and enforce acts of censorship than it had been.

The BBC's defence was that it had a wider responsibility than to the creative self-indulgence of the Pythons: the need to preserve its own freedom and independence. Imposing self-censorship by negotiation was a way of avoiding formal censorship by some outside authority. But the effect was insidious, and caution supplanted creativity, a process paralleled by the way in which administrators of the BBC were building a top-heavy bureaucracy, while the creative personnel were put on short-term contracts that discouraged the sort of initiative that had made *Python* possible in the first place as well as the combativeness that kept it going.

When censorship comes down to a matter of single words, it all becomes very silly, both to the offended and the offending, but the atmosphere in which people are to work is crucial. By the mid-1970s ideas were coming from above, not below, and the sense of censorship and coercion was causing considerable frustration. It was not entirely for these reasons that there was no more *Monty Python* for the BBC after 1974 (as individuals they are very happy to work for the BBC), but there was no encouragement to continue. Ten years after the first show went out, in 1979, the *Radio Times* celebrated *Monty Python*'s anniversary with a big fanfare, the same *Radio Times* that had enraged them with its mistaken – or nonexistent – publicity at the time when they really needed it. It may be that it is part of the Pythons' adversary method to be ungrateful, and there must be many at the BBC who thought that Python was biting the hand that fed it. As their range of interests grew, the Pythons gained the confidence to take a piece out of even bigger hands than the BBC's.

III

'Crude in the extreme'
ITCA

During the arguments over the fourth series of *Monty Python* an exasperated BBC executive told them that if and when Python Productions made their own series, they could say what they liked, but until then they must do what the BBC said. In fact the Pythons had made two television programmes independently, for Germany, and by 1974 they were well established as independent producers of books and records, and, for all the world like rock and roll stars, they had taken *Monty Python* on the road as a stage show. But their eyes were not on television; what interested them was the movies.

The Pythons learned that if the Python method was to be properly applied to any enterprise, they must have proper artistic and financial control. It took experience to establish this fundamental Python principle in the minds of a group who had begun as grateful employees of the BBC, and it took time to establish itself as a financial practice, but it was to be as important as the Python method itself in unifying the group and giving them the freedom to say no to compromise. At the same time as they gained control over their work, however, they also acquired direct responsibility for it. And that involved taking their own decisions about questions of suitability and censorship.

The Pythons began by demonstrating that in artistic matters they knew best. Their natural arrogance inclined them to believe that this was so, but it needed their combined strength to argue their case with the BBC, and they did not always win. In some areas they quickly came to the conclusion that they were better off doing things entirely for themselves. The first record was an early lesson. In 1970, following the success of Series I, the BBC invited them to make a record based on sound tracks from the shows. Not content to leave it at that, the Pythons put in a lot of work to produce a linking script that would exploit (and subvert) the rich possibilities of stereo recording. It was something of a surprise, then, to find themselves one stifling hot summer afternoon before an uninvited audience at the BBC Paris Studio, as though they were taking part in a quiz programme. It was even more of a surprise to discover that their stereo

jokes were to be recorded in mono. With the help of a very patient audience they managed to produce a crude version of a radio show, but from then on they resolved to make their own records. As we shall see, the LPs produced since then have had their share of difficulties, but at least they have been produced to the Pythons' satisfaction.

A major step towards the assertion of artistic control was the formation of Python Productions Ltd in August 1970. The decision to form a company that

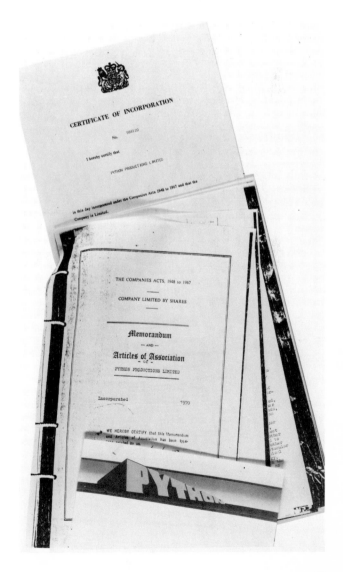

would represent their joint financial interests was prompted by an approach to John Cleese from Victor Lownes of the Playboy Club, who suggested that a feature film could be made out of the television material. At that stage there seemed little chance of the television shows breaking into the American market; *Monty Python* was still unfamiliar to British audiences, and their originality was thought too strong by the TV executives who decided what was safe and acceptable in the United States. A movie, chiefly aimed at the American college circuit, was a way to introduce gently the accents and absurdities of Python. (And a film was a film was a film, a step on from television.) Since Eric Idle's agent, Roger Hancock, was known to have experience in the field, the Pythons sought his advice on forming a company, and one of his associates, John Gledhill, was brought in to manage Python Productions. Gledhill became the first of several non-comedians who have had the thankless task of running the Pythons' joint affairs.

The deal with Victor Lownes went ahead. Directed by Ian MacNaughton, *And Now For Something Completely Different* was filmed in a disused milk depot in October and November 1970, and released a year later. With the budget a mere £80,000 the film was in no way a grand affair, being little more than an assembly of the best material from the first and second series. Nor was there anything wildly outrageous in matters of 'taste and sex', but Victor Lownes found Michael Palin's performance as Ken Shabby too authentically repul-

sive to his finer feelings to keep in the film. When he broke the news to the Pythons after they had all viewed a rough-cut a dispute broke out, and Lownes found himself having to argue his case in a seedy café in Wardour Street, his Rolls-Royce parked incongruously outside. Some Pythons protested that the presence of Shabby would break up the procession of desk-bound sketches that clogged the middle of the movie. (Cleese agreed with Lownes, even though his wife, Connie Booth, featured in the sketch.) Lownes as producer had control over the final shape of the film,

and Ken Shabby coughed his last on the cutting-room floor. Terry Gilliam also had a bitter argument with Lownes over the design of the film's credits. Originally Lownes agreed that the credits should begin with muted typographical elegance, before the mock-Bible-epic *Monty Python* credits came crashing down in typical Gilliam style. (Some prints of the film retain this sequence.) But, as designed by Gilliam, Victor Lownes' name, though elegant, was small. Lownes demanded that his name should also appear in monumental style. Gilliam fought hard against this because it spoiled the visual effect, but the producer remained adamant. In the end Gilliam walked away from the argument and Lownes employed someone else to redesign his credit in large enough letters. Artistic control rarely runs to control over film credits, whatever the contracts say, though Cleese thought this a small price to pay for Lownes's encouragement of the group.

In other fields the existence of Python Productions and the formation of a music publishing company, KGB Music, enabled the Pythons to sign a deal with Charisma Records, and the first production entirely under their own control was *Another Monty Python Record*, released in 1971. But the project that began to bring in financial as well as artistic rewards was *Monty Python's Big Red Book* (in a blue cover) published by Methuen on 1 November 1971. John Gledhill recalls that just as he was about to conclude the contractual negotiations with Methuen, he received a telephone call from the Head of Copyright at the BBC. Was it true that the Pythons were thinking of publishing a book? It was. But surely the BBC owned the rights in this area? Certainly not, and the Head of Copyright should consult the relevant documents. The H. of C. retired to do so, and telephoned Gledhill again the following day. 'I have consulted the files, Mr Gledhill, and you are quite right. You may proceed.' Gledhill thought it redundant to thank him for this unnecessary permission, since he had signed the contract that morning, but he allowed the BBC to be paternalistic to the end.

Just as *And Now For Something Completely Different* taught the Pythons that there were strict limits to actors' and writers' control in the film industry, *Monty Python's Big Red Book*, and its successor in 1973, *The Brand New Monty Python Bok*, taught them the legal constraints on publishing. The Python principle began to enrich them, but the Python method brought them up against obstacles of copyright, obscenity and libel.

The interest of *The Big Red Book* – apart from the fact that it pioneered the now-saturated book-of-the-series market – was the way in which the Pythons were able to have complete control over the contents and make all the editorial and production decisions themselves. Curiously, Terry Gilliam was not anxious to be involved in the design, possibly because he had had enough of lay-outs and paste-ups in the 1960s with his magazine *Help!*. He was not at all sure that the book would sell and Eric Idle, who as the most literary and the most interested became editor, recalls that they had to break into Gilliam's studio to rescue bits of artwork from the animations.

Eric Idle brought in an outside designer, Derek Birdsall, and they constructed the book on the simple principle that they knew in advance the published price, the number to be printed and the maximum production cost per copy. This gave them a budget, and within that budget they could take the decisions they wanted on the proportion of colour to black and white, how much they would cut the pages about and so forth. For *Monty Python's Big Red Book* there was a considerable element of recycled television material, but Idle made every effort to recast it in terms that would parody print in the way that the shows subverted television. Once the other Pythons saw what the possibilities were they contributed criticism, new ideas and new material.

One of the pleasures of Python is the way people like Huw Wheldon, Reginald Bosanquet, Andrew Gardner and others co-operated in contributing to the *Big Red Book*. (Their reward was a very silly launching party, at which there was a prize for every newsreader. Naturally, the Python publicity was self-parody.) The use of real names and faces is an established Python style, and in the case of the newscasters Python Productions was careful to get their agreement first, but copyright in trade names is a more complicated business, particularly where parodies of advertisements are concerned. Most advertisers are delighted to have the extra free publicity, but the copyright laws can be used by the humorless to revenge themselves on the most innocent fun. The Pythons had their first lesson in copyright when they used real trade names, not as objects of satire but to lend authenticity to their Song for Europe, 'Bing Tiddle Tiddle Bong'.

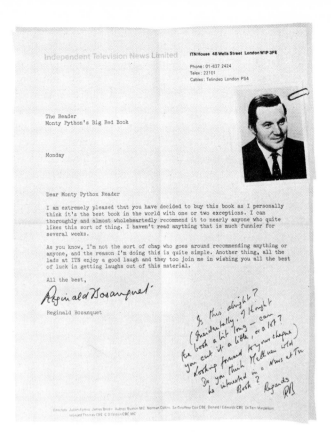

To their surprise, the Pythons received a letter, via Methuen, from the firm from whose sheet music the authenticating advertisements had been taken. Far from being delighted by the extra publicity for their ukele tutors, the firm claimed that this was a serious breach of copyright. Not only that, the use of their advertisements might be taken as an endorsement of 'Bing Tiddle Tiddle Bong', which of course was not the case. The Pythons thought that this reaction was excessive, but an action for an injunction could have stopped sales of the *Big Red Book* just as it was turning out to be a best-seller. After the first 75,000 copies (which were already in the shops when the trouble started), all further printings underwent a tiny change.

A too-close parody of an advertisement for the W. H. Smith–Doubleday-owned book club, the Literary Guild, discouraged the work's selection as a book club edition.

As far as the more serious dangers of problems with obscenity are concerned, British law places the printed word and image in a different position to film and television. The law is in black and white on the statute books (the Obscene Publications Act of 1959, tidied up by the Obscene Publications Act of 1964, the Post Office Act of 1953, the Customs Consolidation Act of 1876), but it is not at all clear how or when the law is going to be applied, and an army of solicitors and barristers is kept busy advising publishers on the law's possible meaning. Publishers have to take their decisions on the strength of informed guesses as to what the police and the Director of Public Prosecutions might do, and what could happen in court. The *Lady Chatterley's Lover* case of 1960 seemed to suggest that serious literature, at least, might not be found obscene by a jury invited to decide whether it had a tendency to deprave or corrupt. But the *Last Exit to Brooklyn* case in 1968 and the *Oz* case of 1971 showed that there were no

guarantees against prosecution. The position is complicated because it is possible under the Obscene Publications Act of 1959 for goods simply to be seized by the police, who can bring them before a magistrate, without a jury, and ask for their destruction. Though juries have been less and less willing to convict, magistrates have felt far less compunction.

Although in 1968 the British publisher of *Last Exit To Brooklyn*, John Calder, thought that serious art and literature were so threatened that he formed the Defence of Literature and the Arts Society, conditions generally have relaxed in Britain over what may be published in books and magazines, particularly as far as images of naked ladies are concerned. H.M. Customs, who have fierce powers to seize and destroy offensive material coming into the country, admit that they would prosecute much of the material actually published in the United Kingdom and openly available on newsagents' shelves. In that respect neither *Monty Python's Big Red Book* nor *The Brand New Monty Python Bok* could have appeared as they did five years earlier, but even in the 1970s the Pythons found that the isolated word could still cause serious trouble.

Customarily, an author's words are his own responsibility.

II. The AUTHOR hereby warrants to the PUBLISHERS that the said work is an original work, has not been published in volume form and that neither the work nor any illustration nor any part thereof is in any way whatever a violation of any existing copyright, that the work contains nothing obscene, indecent, objectionable or libellous, that all statements contained therein purporting to be facts are true, and that he has full power to make this Agreement, and will indemnify the PUBLISHERS against any loss, injury or damage (including any legal costs and expenses and any compensation costs and disbursements paid by the PUBLISHERS on the advice of Counsel to Compromise or settle any claim) occasioned to the PUBLISHERS in consequence of any breach of this warranty.

The Eyre Methuen executive responsible for dealing with Python publications, Geoffrey Strachan, bore, in co-operation with the Pythons, the primary responsibility for negotiating the obstacles of copyright, libel and obscenity that Python books tended to encounter. In 1973 *The Brand New Monty Python Bok* was again edited by Eric Idle, this time designed by Kate Hepburn. She was given a studio in the same building as Eyre Methuen and its parent company Associated Book Publishers, where the comings and goings of the Pythons caused confusion to at least one senior director, who could not believe that these lunatic urchins were the real Pythons of television. On 28 March 1973 Strachan began to send rough proofs of the *Bok* to the firm's solicitor, Michael Rubinstein. By 31 May it began to look as though the *Bok* could emerge with a

clean bill of health, provided, that is, that any prosecution under the Obscene Publications Act brought them in front of a jury rather than a magistrate.

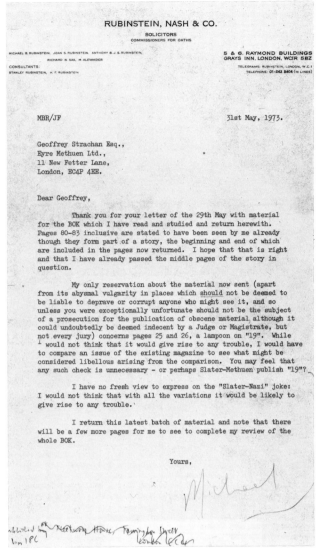

The difficulty for both lawyer and publisher when trying to anticipate trouble over a book is that a lawyer's opinion is still only an opinion, and opinions differ. It is impossible to guarantee against prosecution, except by making the material so innocuous that the question would not arise. When publishing Python, that is hardly the point. Publishers have also to consider that they are not the only ones who can be brought into court to defend their actions. The printer, and indeed the bookseller, is also at risk. The printer's co-operation is vital and, though printers do not wish to be censors, they too must take steps to protect their businesses (businesses often more substantial than those of the publishers they work for). In the case of *Monty Python* it is always prudent to check, and when the printers consulted their lawyers, these took the further precaution of consulting a barrister who specialized in such matters. The barrister took a less relaxed view of obscenity and libel than Michael Rubinstein.

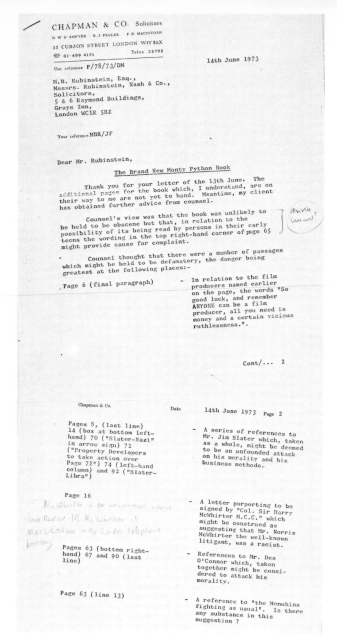

CHAPMAN & CO. Solicitors
D W G SAWYER · B J PEGLER · P D MACINTOSH
15 CURZON STREET LONDON W1Y 8AX
☎ 01-499 4151   Telex 28798

Our reference P/78/73/DM   14th June 1973

M.B. Rubinstein, Esq.,
Messrs. Rubinstein, Nash & Co.,
Solicitors,
5 & 6 Raymond Buildings,
Grays Inn,
London WC1R 5BZ

Your reference MBR/JF

Dear Mr. Rubinstein,

                    The Brand New Monty Python Book

        Thank you for your letter of the 13th June. The
additional pages for the book which, I understand, are on
their way to me are not yet to hand. Meantime, my client
has obtained further advice from counsel.

        Counsel's view was that the book was unlikely to
be held to be obscene but that, in relation to the
possibility of its being read by persons in their early
teens the wording in the top right-hand corner of page 65
might provide cause for complaint.

        Counsel thought that there were a number of passages
which might be held to be defamatory, the danger being
greatest at the following places:-

Page 6 (final paragraph)   - In relation to the film
                                producers named earlier
                                on the page, the words "So
                                good luck, and remember
                                ANYONE can be a film
                                producer, all you need is
                                money and a certain vicious
                                ruthlessness.".

                                            Cont/... 2

Chapman & Co.   Date 14th June 1973 Page 2

Pages 8, (last line)   - A series of references to
14 (box at bottom left-   Mr. Jim Slater which, taken
hand) 70 ("Slater-Nazi"   as a whole, might be deemed
in arrow sign) 72   to be an unfounded attack
("Property Developers   on his morality and his
to take action over   business methods.
Page 71") 74 (left-hand
column) and 92 ("Slater-
Libra")

Page 16   - A letter purporting to be
                                signed by "Col. Sir Harry
                                McWhirter M.C.C." which
                                might be construed as
                                suggesting that Mr. Norris
                                McWhirter the well-known
                                litigant, was a racist.

Pages 63 (bottom right-   - References to Mr. Des
hand) 67 and 90 (last   O'Connor which, taken
line)   together might be consi-
                                dered to attack his
                                morality.

Page 63 (line 13)   - A reference to "the Menuhins
                                fighting as usual". Is there
                                any substance in this
                                suggestion ?

Chapman & Co.   Date 14th June 1973   Page 3

In view of this advice, our client would be very reluctant to
print the work without your client's unqualified assurance in
writing that it believes that our client would have a good
defence to any action or actions for libel brought in relation
to the above-mentioned passages. Please may this be given ?

        Counsel pointed out that the reference to Harrods
on page 92 states that the store is closed at weekends whereas
this is not now the case. We pass this on to avoid the
necessity of a later correction.

                    Yours sincerely,

The first effect of prudence is delay. For publishers a delay in the delivery of books to the shops means that they miss the optimum moment for the largest sales – in this case Eyre Methuen were again aiming for the Christmas market. In June there are many shopping days to Christmas, but printing days are already running out. At Eyre Methuen Strachan decided that it was time to get in touch with the Pythons to see what legal advice they had received. This was easier said than done, however, for Eric Idle had left the convenient studio upstairs and joined the rest of the Pythons in their latest independent venture, a tour of Canada with a stage show. Strachan *was* able to get in touch with the Python lawyers, however, and the opinion of yet another lawyer was sought. The ten-page opinion of Mr Roydon Thomas included this shrewd comment on the in-built protection of the Pythons' commitment to the absurd.

7.

    When one considers "Monty Pythons Flying
Circus" I think one must have regard to its
history and background. The latter is well-
known as a result of the television programmes.
I think one's approach must include recognition
that most people who are likely to read the book
will expect some topics to be treated lightly -
or to be "sent up". This factor is also relevant
when considering the issue of obscenity.

    Another important factor is to recognise and
to stress that the Courts acknowledge the changing
standards and pattern of society. Many magazines
or articles which were published only 10 years ago
and were then considered shocking would not now cause
a head to turn. Bare breasts have been overtaken by
pubic hair.

    I can perhaps illustrate both the above points
by reference to the page Tits'n Bums. In this day
and age I do not think this would be classed as
obscene. It may not be thought very funny - I do
not wish to stray into the realm of critic - but put
in context it does not have the attributes of hard
pornography. Even considered in isolation from the
remainder of the book, I do not think it would be
considered obscene. Turning specifically to the
wording, an argument could perhaps be mounted that
there will only be one Parish Hall in the Parish of
Willesden - there will be other minor churches but
only one Parish Church. Accordingly, there could
only be one Vicar referred to. This is an unreal
approach - akin to, say, the recent "Stop knocking
Neason" campaign. In any event a Plaintiff would
have to link the cover picture with the words on the
cover.

Having tried to reassure themselves, the printers instead found a fresh set of litigious possibilities, and they felt unwilling to go ahead with printing the book.

At the same time, however, Roydon Thomas found yet more dangers in the text, which the Python solicitors conveyed to Michael Rubinstein.

DENTON HALL & BURGIN
SOLICITORS

3, GRAY'S INN PLACE,
GRAY'S INN,
LONDON,
WC1R 5EA.

THE RT. HON. LORD FLETCHER, LL.D.
PATRICK LESLIE BURGIN   MICHAEL F. FLINT
MICHAEL J. BROWN, M.A.   ARTHUR L. MARRIOTT
JOHN R. SALTER, M.A.   CHARLES H. G. GREEN
HENRY E. ST L. KING, M.A.,LL.B.   STEVEN R. BEHARRELL
TIMOTHY L. KIRBY   PETER GLYN-JONES, LL.B.
DONAL P. MOLONEY, LL.B.   N.J.B. COOPER, M.A.,LL.B.
ARTHUR J. BUCK   R.R.C. STOKES, T.D.,M.A.
HUGH CANHAM, LL.M.,PH.D.   ALAN P. WILLIAMS, LL.B.
B. M. KIRKHAM, LL.B.
DAVID J. NORRIS, LL.B.   Associate
J. MICHAEL CATHERALL, M.A.,LL.B.   W. FRANK PROUDFOOT, M.A.
THOMAS F. F. TAYLOR, M.A.

BY HAND

TELEPHONE 01-242 1212 & 01-242 7485
TELEGRAMS BURGINHAL,LONDON, TELEX
CABLES. BURGINHAL,LONDON,W.C.1.
TELEX 263587

21st June 1973

Our Ref: LMH/JB
MBR/BD

M. Rubinstein, Esq.,
Rubinstein Nash & Co.,
5 & 6 Raymond Buildings,
Grays Inn,
London WC1R 5BZ

Dear Mr. Rubinstein,

re: "The Brand New Monty Python Book"

I trust that you will have received opinion from Mr. Roydon Thomas which I sent to you in last nights post. Over night I considered that opinion and I have advised my Clients that the following points give rise to concern in the opinion of this firm:-

1.   The cover page of "16" - We are slightly (but not terribly) worried by the reactions of Messrs Baxter, and Burke to this page.

2.   I have advised my Clients that the most potentially dangerous page is the Egomony Guide and have asked for assurance from them that the addresses have been checked. The same comment applies to Col. Sir Harry McWhirter M.C.C., I have instructed my Clients to check that such a man does not exist.

3.   The article entitled "How to become a Segas Employee" worrys us a little, mostly because we do not know what it is supposed to mean. I have asked my Clients to check whether this is accurate and also whether the expression "set of out worn socio-political theories" has any particular significance.

...ein Esq.,

21st June 1973

- 2 -

...are particularly worried by "masturbators of ...nd the references there to Mr. Alan Brien. I ...ed my Clients that we think it likely that ...ould have an action for damages.

...re also concerned about the advertisement ...don International Hitler Hotel". We think ...t the London International Hotel, Jim Slater, ..., Pan-Am and/or TWA could consider themselves ...this advertisement. (the sign in the advertise-...ure of the Pan-Am and TWA trademarks).

...ing to get in touch with the Authors in ...to them our thoughts and I will let ...s I know whether alterations are going ...to the book, or whether my Clients have decided ...ke the risk.

Phone Alan Brien

Yours sincerely,

Lidsay Harrison

c.c. B. Cook Esq.,
     B.J. Pegler Esq.,

33

On the basis of the advice they had taken, and in the interests of getting the book out in time, both Eyre Methuen and Python Productions Ltd decided to take the risk and give the printers the assurances about libel that they were asking for – which in the case of Eyre Methuen was done the very next day, since they were now desperately anxious that printing should begin.

Unfortunately, Eyre Methuen had forgotten about the small matter of the top right-hand corner of page 65, a reworking of Eric Idle's famous Spanish holiday

. . . miserable pittance they got for the privilege of having a thirty-floor hotel built in their front garden: and he tries to tell you about God, and Churchill and comradeship in the army and he puts his hand on your thigh and starts crying and talking of loneliness and passes out while the tourists titter and the Scotsman at the bar offers you a choice between his drinks bill or your hospital bill and you finally stagger out and get picked up by some English cow who hasn't had it for months, who smells like a distillery and who's leaping out of her clothes in all directions, and she tugs at your belt muttering about holiday romance and all the Spanish brandy she's had so that she's got an alibi in the morning, and then coaxes your brewer's droop into vague interest long enough for her to leap all over you shivering and moaning and biting your ears and squealing "Otto! Otto!" the name of the coach driver on her last package holiday who got so drunk he went up to her room and then had to climb out the window when he saw what the goods were like. . . .

monologue. This was a matter of possible prosecution for obscenity, not libel, and if the top right-hand corner of page 65 did land everybody in court, then assurances and indemnities from the publisher would not get the printers off the hook. Either the printers also took a risk, or the offending item would have to go. But a change had to be agreed to by the Pythons – and there were no Pythons to hand because of the now closing tour of Canada. At last one Python, John Cleese, returned to London and, though strictly Eric Idle was the editor, Strachan appealed to Cleese to give formal agreement to a change. Cleese took the responsibility, looked at the offending page, and just in time for printing schedules, the change to page 65 took place.

With the removal of the word 'penis' the presses were permitted to roll.

The freebooting world of the record industry has not had time to acquire the traditional constraints of publishing, nor is it directly under the institutional restrictions of broadcasting. The connoisseur of coarse language should compare the version of the 'Parrot' sketch on the first, BBC, record and the subsequent version of that and other sketches on the recording of *Monty Python Live at Drury Lane* (1974). Indeed, *Live at Drury Lane* shows that the Theatres Act of 1968 allowed the Pythons to do just about what they liked on stage. Some of the language on the records has caused resistance from retailers who have chosen not to stock risky material, but the Pythons did not run into major trouble with their records until their seventh for

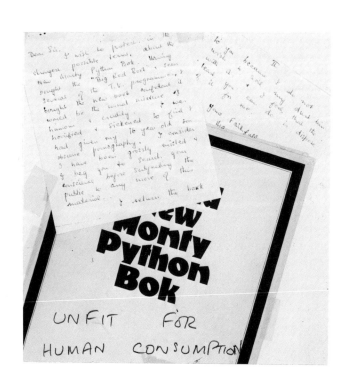

34

Charisma. Being the last under their original contract, it was jokingly titled *Monty Python's Contractual Obligation Album* and packaged as a bootleg LP.

As usual, the Pythons produced their own master tape (this one under the direction of Eric Idle), at André Jaquemin's Redwood Studios and leased the tape to Charisma Records. It was Charisma's job to manufacture and market the LP. Charisma had done well from *Monty Python* and done well by them, going along full tilt with the Pythons' ways, from crossed-out classical record sleeves to triple-banded LPs (a Terry Jones production device). But a Python record had never made it into the Top Ten and this time Charisma's Mike Watts decided to promote the release in October 1980 with television as well as radio advertising on the commercial broadcasting network. The contents of the LP were, as usual, strong and seemed to reflect recent troubles with references to bishops and lawsuits. The proposed commercials were perfectly innocuous, but all broadcast advertising material has to be vetted by the Independent Television Companies Association, an organization that works closely with the Independent Broadcasting Authority's Advertising Control Division to enforce the Code of Advertising Standards and Practice under the Independent Television Act. Charisma's advertising agency made an initial approach to the ITCA – but received this unexpected rebuff, the first of two, both, of course, very proper:

I'm sorry. This contract clearly states you will make 6 L.P.'s. To date you've only made 5.

Graham Chapman

I want to see a solicitor

John Cleese

I am a solicitor

T. Jones

Well... couldn't we just put together some old sketches?

John Cleese

NO! No parrots. No mention of Marcel Proust. No Mrs. Niggerbaiter.

M. Palin

I don't want to make a record

John Cleese

Nonsense, everyone wants to make a record

T. Jones

Do we have a choice?

John Cleese

ugh ... six months or financial ruin through the courts.

G. Chapman

Well I don't know what to say

John Cleese

You never did know how to end a sketch ...
Ladies and Gentlemen.
The new Monty Python
Contractual Obligation L.P.
will be available in record shops from October 5th. With new songs and sketches.
Agreed?

M. Palin

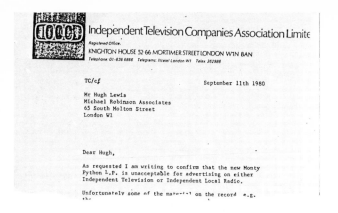

The point must be made absolutely clear that the ITCA refused to allow the commercials (which as a result were never made) not because they were in themselves offensive, but because the *product* they marketed was deemed to be 'crude in the extreme'. Since *Monty Python's Flying Circus* was actually the product of television, and had not been banned there, Mike Watts at Charisma tried to find out just what it was that was so objectionable.

The ITCA also banned Virgin Records retail shops from advertising five Charisma LPs on Capital Radio because the proposed ad featured Mr Souza's innocent *Python* signature tune, 'Liberty Bell' – by implication drawing attention to the *Contractual Obligation Album.* This must be the first time that the band of the

Grenadier Guards has been deemed to be offensive in other than a military role.

After a while the ITCA stopped communicating with Charisma altogether, but they had already unwittingly suggested an advertising slogan, and 'crude in the extreme' became the promotional line in a poster campaign planned for the London Underground. But London Transport has its own censors and Charisma's proposal came back as unacceptable.

It was at this point that Charisma's logo, the Mad Hatter, put on a judge's wig, and they added the jokey seal 'Now a Major Lawsuit'. Little did they know.

In the meantime the BBC picked up what was going on at the ITCA and in the spirit of rivalry gave the *Contractual Obligation Album* plenty of plays, including tracks which had offended the ITCA. Whereas the local commercial radio station in Birmingham, BRMB, banned the LP's single, 'I like Chinese' because it might offend Birmingham's Chinese minority, the record was well liked at the BBC. Charisma's next promotional invention was pairs of underpants (a play on

the usual tee-shirts) bearing the slogan 'Monty Python Sat on My Face', to be sent to world leaders and members of the ITCA as Python's contribution to world peace. Tommy Vance proudly wore his pair on BBC's *Top of the Pops* (on his head). The regular and free publicity from the *Contractual Obligation Album's* advertising problems helped to push it to number thirteen in the sales charts, when the 'major lawsuit' turned out to be for real.

The Pythons were back with 'Bing Tiddle Tiddle Bong', but with a vengeance. Parodies and close allusions, as we saw, must be cleared with the copyright owners. In this case, possibly so as not to alert them to the news that in this case the copyright owner was heard to be strangled, Charisma had cleared the use of John Denver's 'Annie's Song' with John Denver's music publishers but not as a parody. Three weeks after the record was released, Charisma and the Pythons faced a major lawsuit for breach of copyright *and* defamation of (John Denver's) character. The track had to be removed from pressings of the LP and replaced with an announcement that it had disappeared 'on legal advice', but there remained the problem of the record sleeves, where Denver's name was listed. Charisma offered a compromise:

But the threat of further action necessitated more drastic measures:

The irony of the *Contractual Obligation Album* was that although the record failed to reach the Top Ten, the Pythons and Charisma did not lose out from the obstacles placed in its path; in fact the costs of promoting it turned out to be a lot less than if television commercials had been allowed to be made in the first place.

The punchline, though, must go to Boots Ltd, who proved that not all retailers refuse a challenge. Seized with the Python spirit, they produced at their own expense this special sticker:

The contents may offend some Listeners

Books and records have provided Python Productions with a steady income, besides lessons in their legal obligations. But the Python principle first came of age in 1974 with their second feature film, *Monty Python and the Holy Grail*. This was altogether a more ambitious project than *And Now For Something Completely Different*, both artistically and financially. The script was a specially written complete story that took the Pythons out of the contemporary middle-class milieu of the television screen into a much more expansive and decorative early Middle Ages. The financing of the film was unusual, for

such film-making interests as there are in Britain were not interested in the unproven, unformulaic Pythons. Instead they found their own producer, Mark Forstater, and formed their own film company, Python (Monty) Pictures. Most of the finance for the film came from the theatre impresario Michael White, and an unlikely group of 'angels' helped to put up the money, including Charisma, Island Records, Led Zeppelin and Pink Floyd. The main financial contribution from the Pythons was to make the film for virtually nothing, in moderate discomfort, and to defer their fees until such time as *The Holy Grail* made a profit. The total cost of production was just over £229,000, and 'democracy gone mad' demanded that there should be two directors, Terry Jones and Terry Gilliam, with everybody acting and everybody contributing their criticism.

The Python method produced a film that was at times violent and ordurous, but also very beautiful. It was also more original in conception and execution than anything being made by the large, orthodox film companies, and considerably cheaper. But films, too, must confront institutional constraints. In the United Kingdom the relevant authority was the British Board of Film Censors, whose detailed functions are discussed in a later chapter, and who are important here only because their assessment of the film could affect the size of audience permitted to see the

Pythons' work. An 'X' certificate would limit the audience to 18-year-olds and older, and naturally the Pythons wanted to be seen by as many people as possible. Precaution was taken during filming to make 'cover shots' to provide alternative words and images if cuts were demanded.

August 5th, 1974.

Dear Mike,

The Censor's representative, Tony Kerpel, came along to Friday's screening at Twickenham and he gave us his opinion of the film's probable certificate.

He thinks the film will be **AA**, but it would be possible, given some dialogue cuts, to make the film an **A** rating, which would increase the audience. (AA is 14 and over, and A is 5 - 14).

For an '<u>A</u>' we would have to:

Lose as many <u>shits</u> as possible

Take <u>Jesus Christ</u> out, if possible

Lose "I fart in your general direction"

Lose "the <u>oral sex</u>"

Lose "oh, fuck off"

Lose "We make castanets out of your testicles"

I would like to get back to the Censor and agree to lose the <u>shits</u>, take the odd <u>Jesus Christ</u> out and lose <u>Oh fuck off</u>, but to retain 'fart in your general direction', 'castanets of your testicles' and 'oral sex' and ask him for an 'A' rating on that basis.

Please let me know as soon as possible your attitude to this.

Yours sincerely,

<u>Mark Forstater</u>

In the interest of a wider audience (and possibly a quicker payment of their deferred fees) the Pythons agreed to negotiate. Although the then Secretary of the Board of Censors, Stephen Murphy, did remark in passing to Michael Palin that 'oral sex is a problem', he was chiefly concerned about the element of violence in the film. Terry Jones remembers Murphy coming to the cutting room where the film was being edited to supervise personally the removal of just two frames from the gory scene between King Arthur and the Black Knight. Jones thought it was awfully nice of him to take the trouble. *Monty Python and the Holy Grail* was released in April 1975, proudly bearing an 'A' certificate.

Monty Python and The Holy Grail proved a watershed in the group's career. On the one hand *Monty Python* stepped out confidently from beneath the wing of the BBC. They were already experienced producers of their own books, records and stage shows, and the *Holy Grail* registered a successful complete transition from the small to the big screen. On the other hand, the continuous interaction of the group over the previous five years had virtually exhausted their mutual patience and each wanted to go off and do things on his own. Ironically, this was much easier for them individually because of their collective reputation. Michael Palin has described the eighteen months or so after the completion of the fourth television series as 'a period in the wilderness', but the point about the wilderness (an unconsciously Biblical allusion) is that people return from it with their will made stronger. The period from 1969 to 1974 established certain firm principles of conduct among the Pythons. Even before they had a chance to apply these to fresh work, they were to be put to a severe legal test.

BISHOP

Yea... as Raymond Chandler said: It was one
of those days when Los Angeles felt like a
rock hard fig -

BRIG.

Oh Brian, let's stop pretending ...

BISHOP

Oh ... yea ... as Dirk Bogarde said in his
autobiography ...

BRIG.

Oh, let's stop this futile pretence... I've
always been moderately fond of you ...

BISHOP

Well to be quite frank Brigadier ... one can't
walk so closely with a chap like you for so
long without ... feeling ... well ... feeling
something deep down inside, even if it isn't
... anything ... very much.

BRIG.

Well! Splendid ... Brian ... er ... well
there's not much we can do really.

BISHOP

Not on television ... no ...

(PAUSE)

BRIG.

They are a lot more permissive than they used
to be ...

BISHOP

Oh yes ... I suppose ... one has to draw the
line somewhere ...

BISHOP

Yes ...

(PAUSE)

BRIG.

Well ... Take another letter. Dear Sir, I
wish to protest in the strongest possible
terms...

(FADE AND GO INTO ANIMATION.
ANIMATION TAKES US INTO:)

IV

'Each episode will be shown in its entirety'

BBC Enterprises

Monty Python Series IV went out on BBC2 in the autumn of 1974. It was not a happy time for the group; for one thing, John Cleese's refusal to take part in the fourth series threw them off balance. Without Cleese, the BBC would only agree to make six shows and insisted that the words *Flying Circus* be dropped from the title.

Viewers disagreed about the effect of John Cleese's absence, but whatever doubts there were about the group's future in British television, their career was starting all over again in America. And in America the Pythons were to find themselves making legal history.

A key part of the BBC's empire is known as BBC Enterprises: its job is to exploit BBC programmes any way it can, by marketing books, records, television characters, tee-shirts and whatever else comes to hand. Above all, it tries to sell BBC programmes abroad. The sale of programmes makes money for the writers and performers, and the best place to sell them is in the United States. The nearest thing to the BBC in America is the PBS, the Public Broadcasting Service on Channel 13; it is not like the BBC in that it is a series of local stations, mainly in the big cities, and is financed by a mixture of grants, sponsorship and private subscriptions, but it is like the BBC in that it does not exist to make a profit, and it tries to educate as well as entertain. With these limitations the PBS cannot pay as well as the three major American networks, ABC, NBC and CBS, nor does it have anything like their coverage or power, but it has always been a good customer of the BBC.

In July 1974 KERA in Dallas, Texas, became the first American public service television station to broadcast *Monty Python*, and Gumbies and Pepperpots began to shock and delight a new audience. *Python* was already known to some young Americans, particularly college students, through word of mouth, records and books, and the film *And Now for Something Completely Different*, but TV programme planners had feared that the Britishness of the language and the domesticity of the references would make *Python* incomprehensible. As usual the executives under-estimated their audience,

and *Python* quickly became the most popular programme on Channel 13. By the end of 1975, with *The Holy Grail* helping the cult, some 130 PBS stations were broadcasting *Python* shows, and even two local commercial stations, in Las Vegas and Houston, had taken *Python* on.

The highly competitive major networks are quick to exploit a trend, and in the spring of 1975 Bob Shanks, a vice-president in charge of late-night programming for ABC Entertainment, the television arm of the American Broadcasting Company, began to sound out the possibility of *Python* being bought and broadcast by ABC.

BBC Enterprises are only part of a series of links between the original programme makers and whoever eventually transmits their shows abroad; quite often the originators have no idea when their work is being broadcast or where. In America, the BBC for tax reasons does not trade directly, but uses an associated company, Time Life Films, and this long chain between creator and consumer was to prove very significant. At ABC, Bob Shanks's first idea was to take the thirteen episodes of *Monty Python's Flying Circus* Series III and produce a compilation that would fit the ninety-minute programme space for which he was responsible, ABC's late-night *Wide World of Entertainment*. (The programme was aimed at a youth audience, and tended to feature recordings of rock concerts.) The proposal from Bob Shanks was passed along the chain of communications to the Pythons, who turned it down. They felt a strong commitment to the Public Service system that had risked taking them on in the first place, and they had an idea of what the Pythons presented on an American commercial network might look like.

Still, the reputation of the Pythons continued to grow in America, and ABC still persisted. A possible solution to the problem was that Time Life Films had not yet sold the rights to *Monty Python* Series IV, whose six shows could in theory fit two ninety-minute programme slots. On 25 June Bill Miller of Time Life Films in New York drafted the following cable to Peter Dimmock of BBC Enterprises in London:

You will be happy to hear that we have completed a deal with

ABC's WIDE WORLD OF ENTERTAINMENT for two 90-minute MONTY

PYTHON specials ~~based on~~ using the six half-hour shows titled MONTY

PYTHON (Series IV). This will not conflict with our prior

PBS sales since the series has never been sold before.XXX ABC

has also agreed to give on-air credit to the PBS series MONTY

PYTHON'S FLYING CIRCUS.

                                    Regards, Bill

The draft shows that there was some vagueness about what exactly would be done with *Python*'s material, and on the following day Christine Condon at BBC Enterprises cabled back:

HAVE SEEN YOUR TELEX JUNE 25. RE SALE OF MONTY PYTHON TO ABC'S WILD WORLD OF ENTERTAINMENT. CAN YOU PLEASE CONFIRM THAT EACH 90 MINUTE SPECIAL WILL CONTAIN 3 OF THE PRGS STRUNG TOGETHER AND NOT 2 90-MINUTE'S MADE UP OF EXTRACTS FROM THE SIX PROGS. APPRECIATE SOONEST REPLY.

Bill Miller's assistant answered on 27 June:

Yes, each 90-minute special will consist of three programs strung together. However, there may be certain deletions since they are subject to U.S. broadcast standards and practices code. Regards.

This satisfied BBC Enterprises, for when Jill Foster, at that time agent for Palin, Jones, Chapman and Gilliam, wrote to Peter Dimmock on 1 August asking for confirmation that no alterations would be made, he replied: 'I have been assured by our people in New York that each episode will be shown in its entirety.' But the question still nagged Jill Foster, and she did some arithmetic:

Thank you for your letter of 6th August concerning the American sale of MONTY PYTHON SERIES IV. I was perfectly satisfied with your answer until, in my bath yesterday, it occurred to me that out of this ABC slot of ninety minutes, something in the region of twenty-four minutes will be devoted to commercials. How then I wonder can each episode be shown in its entirety?

The answer came back from BBC Enterprises that they did not know what the position was about commercials or sponsorship: 'We can only reassure you that ABC have decided to run the programmes "back to back", and that there is a firm undertaking not to segment them.'

The first Monty Python *Wide World of Entertainment* was transmitted by ABC between 11.30 p.m. and 1 a.m. on 3–4 October, 1975.

Because they were all in Britain at the time, the Pythons did not see the ABC show until their American manager, Nancy Lewis, came to London at the end of November, bringing with her a recording of the programme. American and British television systems are technically incompatible, so the only way they could actually see what was on the tape was to arrange a special viewing in a back room of Studio 99's video-showroom in Fairfax Road. The Pythons got a surprise. Not only did the ninety-minute tape include twenty-four minutes of commercials, the material had been cut up and rearranged, and, it was clear, censored. The cuts and changes became obvious in the very first minutes, for the show began with an opening edited from the last programme in the series, number 6. Originally the episode had a running theme of a Party Political Broadcast, but the opening announcement that this was to be a broadcast on behalf of the Liberal Party had disappeared. Instead, the show began moments later as the camera explored the

kitchen of the awful Garibaldi family of Droitwich, eating breakfast while an irrelevant sports commentary droned on on the radio, until Mrs Garibaldi ironed the transistor flat and hung it with the cat and other

Pratt, Pratt... back to Pratt again...

(MRS GARIBALDI IRONS RADIO FLAT)

MR GARIBALDI

I like this Ano-Weet, it really unclogs me.

MRS GARIBALDI

Oh do be careful!

RALPH

Sorry Mum.

MR GARIBALDI

I mean a lot of the others say they unclog you, but I didn't have a single bowel movement with those Recto-Puffs.

(RALPH KNOCKS OVER ANO WEET PACKET WITH POPE SPECIAL OFFER)

RALPH

Now - oh, sorry Mum - if we lived in Rhodesia there'd be someone to mop that up for you.

VALERIE

Don't be bleeding stupid. If you lived in bleeding Rhodesia, you'd be out at bleeding fascist rallies every bleeding day. You're a bleeding racist you bleeding are.

MR GARIBALDI

Language!

VALERIE

Well, he gets on my sodding wick.

MR GARIBALDI

That's better.

(PAUSE)

MR GARIBALDI

The best stuff I ever had was that stuff they used to have before the war. Wilkinson's Number 8 Laxative Cereal. Phew! That one went through you like a Ferrari!

(DOORBELL RINGS)

MRS GARIBALDI

Now who can that be at this time of day?

MR GARIBALDI

If it's the man to empty the Elsan, tell him

it's in the hall.

MRS GARIBALDI

Right dear.

MR GARIBALDI

And make sure he holds it the right way up.

RALPH

Dad?

(MAN COMES OUT OF CUPBOARD)

MAN

Yeah?

RALPH

No. No my dad.

MAN

Oh.

(MAN RE-ENTERS CUPBOARD)

RALPH

Dad, Dad why is Rhodesia called Rhodesia...

oh, sorry Dad

(SCENE IN HALL BETWEEN MRS GARIBALDI AND MAN

IN SUIT MAKING KARATE MOVEMENTS)

MRS GARIBALDI

No, no, no thank you, not today, thank you,

thank you for calling.

MR GARIBALDI

Who was that?

MRS GARIBALDI (RE-ENTERING)

The Liberal Party candidate darling. What

have you done?

RALPH (HOLDING SMASHED SINK)

I'm sorry Mum, I was just washing up.

MRS GARIBALDI

Go and sit down.

RALPH

Mum, Mum, why is Rhodesia called Rhodesia?

MR GARIBALDI

Do you remember Go-Eezi? They were hopeless

household objects on the washing line. This was the cue for dialogue, but forty-five seconds suddenly disappeared from the sketch, and the doorbell rang.

Throughout the tape bits of *Monty Python* appeared to have fallen off. No awful lady wiped her feet on the bread, her awful son no longer tucked into corn plasters. The Brigadier and the Bishop began their prophetic dialogue quoted on page 40, but were cut off before getting anywhere. Python shows have never been celebrated for their continuity, but they have a rhythm and an inner logic of reference that makes the inconsequences consequential. The compilation used much of the fifth episode, subtitled 'Mr Neutron', which featured an American Supreme Commander who is bent on the total destruction of the world in the interest of frightening everybody, but suffers from a secret fear of his own body odour. (The joke is purely visual.)

Whether out of sensitiveness to the American supreme command, whose troops had been finally bundled out of Vietnam that April, or to the cosmetic companies whose deodorant ads filled in for the missing bits of *Monty Python*, the joke almost completely disappeared. Absurdest of all, the Pythons' own euphemism, 'naughty bits' had been bleeped, making the joke crude instead of funny.

The Pythons were angry – Michael Palin wrote in his diary at the time that ABC had managed to make the BBC's censors 'look like pioneering liberals'. Their objection was not simply that their shows had been sanitized, but that their carefully constructed jokes – particularly those like the American Supreme Commander who stripped progressively throughout the show – were destroyed. Terry Jones summed up in a letter to Jill Foster:

We were all absolutely appalled at what ~~theyid~~ someone had done to our shows. Not only had they removed ~~the~~ many of the best bits, they'd left in things which (with the ~~cuts~~ cuts they'd made) were weak,~~x~~ ~~puxti~~ pointless and unfunny. Quite honestly the show made us look berks and could have done us no good at all. A fact born out ~~x~~ by the bad feed-back we've had from fans over there.

Our main concern at this moment is twofold:

1) To disociate ourselves from the show that has already gone out.

2) to prevent the next show going out or, if we really cannot, to remove our names and the name of Monty Python from it.

The first job was to find out when the next compilation was scheduled for transmission by ABC, and what ABC had done with it. At the same time they got in touch with the BBC, and their London solicitors. Nancy Lewis returned to New York, where she learned that the second show was due to go out on 26 December. On 9 December the Pythons asked for a delay so that they could view the tape, possibly even edit it themselves, but ABC refused. The BBC were not willing to do anything (and in any case probably could not have done anything anyway) and with so little time in hand the only way to stop the show was to go to law. On 12 December Robert C. Osterberg of Abeles, Clark and Osterberg, New York attorneys, took on the case.

THIS MAILGRAM IS A CONFIRMATION COPY OF THE FOLLOWING MESSAGE:

2127550812 MGM TDMT NEW YORK NY 100 12-12 0548P EST
ZIP
AMERICAN BROADCASTING CO, ATTN LEGAL DEPT
1330 AVE OF THE AMERICAS
NEW YORK NY 10001
OUR CLIENTS, COPYRIGHT OWNERS OF THE MONTY PYTHON SCRIPTS WHO ARE THE
INDIVIDUALS PERFORMING AS MONTY PYTHON HAVE RETAINED US TO ENFORCE
THEIR RIGHTS WITH RESPECT TO THE PROPOSED MONTY PYTHON SPECIAL TO BE
BROADCAST BY YOU DECEMBER 26 1975. OUR CLIENTS ADVISE YOU MADE
UNAUTHORIZED CUTS IN THE CONTENTS OF THE PROGRAM AND THAT YOU REFUSED
TO RECOGNIZE THEIR RIGHTS TO PREVENT THE SAME. FAILURE TO RESTORE ALL
MATERIAL TO PROGRAMS AS ORIGINALLY CREATED FOR PURPOSES OF YOUR
BROADCAST IMPELS US TO FORTHWITH SEEK INJUNCTIVE RELIEF

The Pythons' first priority was to stop the ABC transmission on 26 December, the second was to regain control of their material. The first could be achieved if a judge agreed to issue an injunction that would hold up transmission, but he would only do so if the lawyers could make out that they had a good case that would justify a full hearing. They decided to argue on three grounds: first, that the Pythons' copyright had been infringed because their original agreement with the BBC only allowed the BBC to make minor alterations to the scripts, and then only before the programmes were recorded, and everything had to be done by agreement. ABC had made major changes without the group's agreement and was proposing to transmit the new version against their wishes. They therefore, claimed $500,000 damages from ABC. Second, ABC was proposing to transmit something called 'Monty Python' which the Pythons did not recognize as their own. This was a misdescription of the programme, and illegal under the United States Lanham Act, which forbids passing off inferior products as the genuine article by using forged labels or false descriptions. Third, ABC's show was such a mutilation of the Pythons' original work that to put it out under their name would ruin their professional reputation, and so amounted to unfair competition.

There was already something pythonesque about a group of writers pleading to be kept off national network television; it was a further twist to argue that the Pythons as presented by ABC would be unfairly competing with themselves. Still, the lawyers thought it worth another $500,000 damages.

The Python attorneys filed their case on 15 December in the United States District Court for the Southern District of New York. On the following day ABC's lawyer Clarence Fried of Hawkin, Delafield and Wood filed a preliminary reply, arguing that the agreement between the BBC and Time Life Films (that long line of communication) gave them every right to insert commercials and make 'applicable censorship'. They denied that there was any misdescription under the Lanham Act. The case was slated to Judge Morris E. Lasker, and the two sides had a discussion in the judge's chambers. Since they came out without any agreement, a full hearing of the case for an injunction was arranged for Friday 19 December, just seven days before the second show was due to go out.

With a date for a hearing fixed, Terry Gilliam, as an American citizen, was bound to give evidence. He asked Michael Palin to keep him company, and they flew together to New York two days before the hearing. They had a series of meetings with their lawyers, and ran through what they would have to say in court. ABC was still refusing to let anyone see the tape of the second show, but on the last day before the hearing they suddenly relented. Sensing that there might be a chance of a settlement, Palin and Gilliam, flanked by their lawyers Robert Osterberg and Ina Meibach,

travelled up to the twenty-first floor of the ABC building, and were ushered into a small, softly furnished viewing room. Bob Shanks was there, backed by the head of ABC's Standards and Practices Department and a lady lawyer. The Standards and Practices Department was responsible for making the cuts in the shows, and before viewing the tape the Python party was handed a list of cuts made in the second show. Just looking at the list was enough to make Palin and Gilliam want to walk out, but they were persuaded to view the tape. There followed a tense session of negotiations, with ABC's lawyer desperately trying to get a settlement. Were the Pythons ready to edit the show themselves? Yes, but they would edit for comedy, not for censorship. When they got down to discussing the use of the word 'tit' it became clear that the two sides could not agree. The matter would have to be settled in court.

The Federal Court House in Foley Square at the southern tip of Manhattan has a pillared, neo-classical façade with a wide sweep of steps leading up to the entrance. To the Pythons, it looked as though it might have been built as the set for the opening of a court room drama – except that this *was* a court room drama. To add a touch of grim black and white atmosphere, it was ten degrees below in the square, and the nervous Pythons were glad of the early morning shot of Bourbon they had taken with the last, reluctant 8 a.m. run-through of their testimony. Their lawyers had tried to outline to them what they should say in court, but privately Palin and Gilliam agreed that they would do best if they stayed themselves.

The court room itself was kinder and warmer than they expected, a long narrow room lit by the tall windows of the façade, below which were the empty benches for a jury. The entrance was opposite the jury box, to the right was the high wooden desk of the judge, with the chair for witnesses beside him. Immediately below his desk sat the clerk and the court recorder, facing them was the broad table for the plaintiffs, at which Palin, Gilliam and Nancy Lewis sat with Osterberg, his assistant Raymond Brody, and Ina Meibach. Immediately behind them – and so making it difficult sometimes for the plaintiffs to know what was going on – was the table for the defence. At the far end of the room, facing the judge, were the public benches.

If this was to be a court room drama, then the principal players – the lawyers – were slightly miscast. Robert Osterberg was short, blond-haired, in his mid-thirties. Michael Palin remembers him as a 'fit, tidy, bland sort of man, with the eyes and smile – but unfortunately nothing else – of Kirk Douglas'. Opposing Kirk Douglas was Milton Friedman, for that is how Michael Palin recalls ABC's lawyer Clarence Fried. The *New Yorker* writer who covered the hearing, Hendrik Hertzberg, described him as 'a natty turnip of a man whose comically serious face was punctuated by a

pince-nez'. The Pythons thought of him as a wrinkled prune. It was Fried who provided the only truly dramatic moment in the hearing when in the afternoon, quivering with emotion, he accused the Pythons of 'coming into court with unclean hands'. The Pythons, he claimed, were only in court because they wanted to create publicity for their live appearances at the New York City Center in three weeks time. Unfortunately he had got his facts wrong, the appearances were *for* three weeks, and were not due for another four months. Presiding over the hearing was the genial, honey-voiced Judge Lasker, who surprised the Pythons by not wearing the black robe they had learned to expect from *Perry Mason* or *The Defenders*. Judge Lasker was scrupulously fair, relaxed and ready to smile. He admitted that he had seen several *Monty Python* shows on Channel 13, as well as *The Holy Grail*. The Pythons wondered if he had been watching Channel 13 the night before, when WNET New York had put out the episode from Series III featuring a beauty contest for judges.

This time the Pythons were in a real, not a joke court, and though the drama stayed low key, there was tension because everyone, including the judge, knew that a decision had to be taken quickly about an injunction. The point at issue was not directly one of censorship: it was a matter of property, ownership and money. The Pythons, as the creators of the property in question, felt that they had a right to control what was done with their own material, and their original contract with the BBC conceded that. ABC, as the indirect employers of *Monty Python*, and directly as renters of a video-tape supplied by Time Life Films, felt they could do what they liked with what they were paying for, and their agreement with Time Life Films conceded that. Judge Lasker commented at the beginning of the trial: 'It seems to me that it may be one of those unhappy situations in which both parties have proceeded entirely in good faith by walking right by each other, and the question is what a court of equity should do under such circumstances.'

The Pythons could – and did – argue that their material had been damaged by ABC's editing on a purely technical level. Not only had the rhythm been lost and what they saw as good sketches made pointless or incomprehensible, the sound track that resulted had an audience that laughed at jokes that were no longer there, and sound effects out of step with the pictures. But it was clear that the editing was also censorship. ABC had not simply taken the best material from ninety minutes of *Python* to produce a brilliant sixty-six minutes. They had chosen the sixty-six minutes which they thought would be most acceptable – or least offensive – to their audience. In fact the actual editing was done by Time Life Films, not ABC, who paid Time Life a fee for doing it, but the cuts were asked for by the Standards and Practices Department of ABC. Their worry was not just about the

[handwritten annotations at top:] (1) Ho'oain accurate transcription out by segrach a minclia No 8

Private dick. (13)

Graham hanging out watching 18

(23) Bicycle eliminated.

ABC Special No. 2

Used - "L.E. War" (Show 3)

n title plus lead-in of 1:09 moved up from approximately
head of program for program identification purposes.
over lead-in scenes removed to delete such phrases
one man's love for another in drag," and "the secret
uals."

script pps 32-34.

p 25-28

scene in war office regarding trivializing of war
starting at approximately 4:40 6 seconds removed in four separate cuts
to remove expressions "Good Lord," "Good God," "Oh My God," and "Bastards." *pps 15, 16 17,*

3. In military trial scene, cut of 1:40 starting approximately 2:27 into
scene to delete entire reference to special gaiters presented to soldier by
regiment for "sexually obliging them." Phrases deleted include: "He used
to make them happy in little ways," "He used to oblige them," "Did he
touch them?," "He used to ram things up their - - - ."

as coarse and subjective interpretation of intention.

pps 25-28

4. Fourteen seconds deleted at end of military trial sequence to delete
shots of men showing backsides to camera as well as obscene arm gestures. *p. 30.*

edge? Vaudra

5. In montage sequence of war (2:21 long) including main title of show,
moved to head of special, with 1:12 removed to delete audio references
as itemized in paragraph one above and certain visuals: navy officer
dressed as woman and naked man playing piano. *(the naked man here was used in all 13 of the 3rd Python series seen throughout U.S.)*

6. In skit of television programmers two separate cuts (:06 total) made to
delete "They must be damn new" and "Up your mother next door."

7. Final 1:38 of skit of television programmers, beginning with entrance of
man in wheelchair with sword in head, deleted to eliminate offensive
references to handicapped individuals. Also deleted was replay of
television program showing members of military court with backsides to
camera. *pps 46-49*

8. Animated sequence of grumpy man trying to sleep. 9 seconds deleted to
remove lines "God!" and two "hells" from "What in hell's going on." *cut among misgobbledy*

9. Scene of upper class family in drawing room discussing "tinny" words.
:03 deleted from beginning of sequence to remove two "damns" from
"Croquet hoops look damn pretty" and "Croquet hoops look frightfully
damn pretty."

dear

10. In same sequence 1:06 removed starting with "Intercourse.", "Later,",
to delete section devoted to words with sexual references including
"pert thighs," "erogenous zone" (repeated three times), "tit, tit, tit,
tinny," Accompanying video of father being aroused by these words and
mother dousing him with bucket of cold water also eliminated in this
cut. *pps 56-58*

sexual obsession water is thrown over him

11. Final skit in "L.E. War" of two women watching TV. Several cuts total-
ing :53 deleted to eliminate repeated scenes of woman remotely control-

this is missed, we still get why?

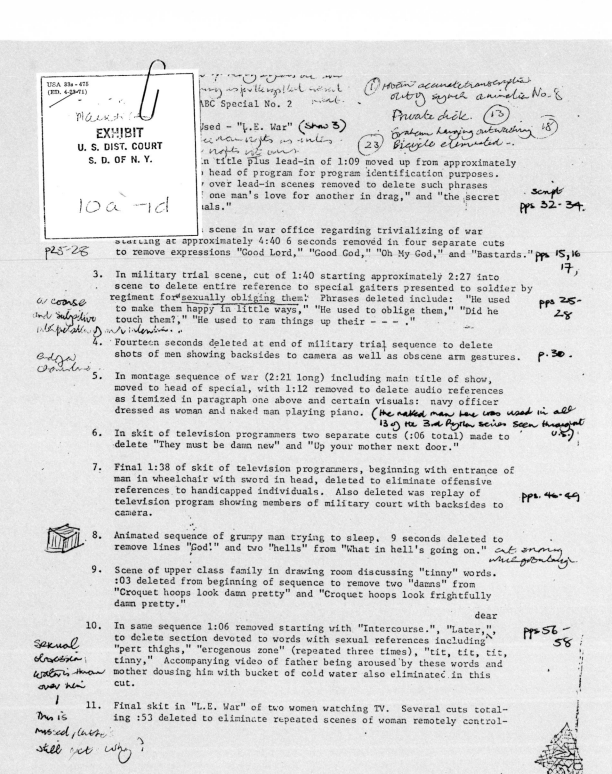

audience, but also the possible reaction of the Federal Communications Commission, which supervises all broadcasting in the United States.

The Standards and Practices Department were the censors, and since the BBC's agreement with Time Life gave Time Life the right to carry out 'applicable censorship' they were doing no more than their job. Exhibit 10 was the three-page list of cuts they had handed Palin and Gilliam the day before.

Asked whether he thought this was an accurate list of the cuts, Michael Palin replied firmly, 'No.' He went on to argue that the censors had been doing rather more than their job, and had revealed something of their minds in the process.

OSTERBERG: Will you give us an example of what you are referring to?

PALIN: An example of where it is just inaccurate is in the very first edit—

THE JUDGE: No. 1?

PALIN: Number 1, the words 'The Secret Loves for Bi-Sexuals.' In fact, in the script, as it is, it is 'The Secret Love for Algy the Bi-Sexual Navigator', which, you know, introduces another element. Just saying 'The secret love for bi-sexuals', he is not what what we said and I think alters our intention.

Having argued that the cuts as described by ABC were in themselves a misrepresentation of what the Pythons had done, Palin was asked to move on to the main question: was the programme as edited by ABC a misrepresentation of their work? The answer was an emphatic yes, and in explaining what he meant, he showed how censorship and mutilation went together.

PALIN: For a start, say, taking point 3, "in military trial scene, cut of 1.40 starting approximately 2.27 into scene to delete entire reference to special gaiters presented to soldier by regiment for 'sexually obliging them'." The words 'sexually obliging them', by the way, were put in by ABC. They don't occur in the script. At any rate it makes a nonsense of the sketch. The sketch is briefly about a court martial in which a counsel is trying to cross-examine a deserter. The judge keeps picking him up on the tiniest little points. Every time he is trying to get through to this deserter—

THE JUDGE: Are there still such judges?

PALIN: Only in our fantasy minds, Your Honour. The sketch is about the progressive irritation of the counsel. He is trying to put questions, perfectly ordinary questions, also in this very formal court set-up, to this deserter. He goes on, he talks about, mentions a town, Basingstoke and the judge picks him up on Basingstoke. 'Where is Basingstoke?' He is getting really mad. So then at one point he says, 'The deserter had in his posses-

GENERAL

No, that's not it... carry on.

FAWCETT

With respect sir, I shall seek to prove that Sapper Walters, being in possession of the following... One Lee-Enfield rifle, one pair of boots, value £3 7/6d... one pair of serge trousers, value £2 3/6d... one pair of gaiters value £68 10/-... one...

GENERAL

£68 10/- for a pair of gaiters?

FAWCETT (DISMISSIVELY)

They were special gaiters, sir.

GENERAL

Special gaiters?

FAWCETT

Yes, they were made in France. One beret costing 14 shillings, one pair of -

GENERAL

What was special about them?

FAWCETT (DISMISSIVELY)

Oh... (HE CAN HARDLY BE BOTHERED TO REPLY)... they were made of special fabric. The buckles were made of empire silver instead of brass. The total value of the uniform was -

GENERAL

Why was he wearing special gaiters?

FAWCETT (GETTING IRRITATED)

They were a presentation **pair**, from the Regiment, sir. The total value of the -

GENERAL

Why did they present him with a special pair of gaiters?

FAWCETT

Sir, I hardly feel it is relevant to the case, whether **his** gaiters were presented or not.

GENERAL

I think the court will be able to judge that

for themselves. <u>Why</u> did the Regiment present

the accused with a special pair of gaiters?

FAWCETT (STIFLING HIS IMPATIENCE)

He... he used to do things for them. The

total value –

GENERAL

What things?

FAWCETT (EXASPERATED)

He... used to oblige them, sir.

GENERAL

Oblige them?

FAWCETT

Yes sir. The <u>total value</u> of the entire –

GENERAL

How did he oblige them?

FAWCETT

What sir?

GENERAL

How did he <u>oblige</u> them?

FAWCETT (MORE AND MORE IRRITATED)

He made them... he made them happy in little

ways, sir. The value **therefore** could not have

been **LESS** than –

GENERAL

Did he touch them at all?

FAWCETT

Sir! I submit this is totally irrelevant!

GENERAL

I want to know how he made them happy.

FAWCETT

He used to shove things up their –

GENERAL

Alright! Alright! No need to <u>spell</u> it out!

(RATHER AT A LOSS) What, er, what **does** the,

er... prisoner have to say?

sion at the time he deserted one Lee-Enfield rifle, one pair of special gaiters, one large tin—' He said 'What were the special gaiters?' They are just gaiters he was given.' Anyway he goes back to the interrogation. The judge keeps coming in on these gaiters, trying to establish why these gaiters were special. He said 'Well, they were given as a token of thanks by the regiment.' 'Yes, yes.' 'Now, did you on this date—' 'And why were they given as a token of thanks?' 'Well they used to make him happy' and he tries to go on. Again the judge comes in, 'In which way did they try to make him happy?'

CLARENCE FRIED: Your Honour, this is very amusing and interesting, but I think this is off the track. The only question is what the effect of that is.

THE JUDGE: Mr Palin is trying to tell me what the original was like so he can tell me what the effect of the excision will be. Overruled. Go ahead. I am not sitting here just because I am amused, although I am amused.

PALIN: At any rate, he keeps going on and the counsel keeps trying to use euphemisms to reply to the judge's constant and persistent little irritating interferences, until at the end the counsel is driven to the point where he is saying, 'They used to make him happy.' 'How did they make him happy?' 'They used to make him content in little ways.' 'What little ways?' 'Your Honour, I really think this is not for this court.' 'No, I want to find out.'

In the end he said 'He used to shove things up their—' At which point the judge interrupts. But the whole point, the validity of that sketch was that it gets to that point, that the court – the whole court business absolutely breaks down and it has an absurd ending.

The sketch as ABC wanted to put it out would end before any of the gaiters bit is mentioned, and therefore we submit it makes it a very ordinary, bland, dull, sketch, without any of the essence of Python in it.

THE JUDGE: Right, I understand.

It was the matter of mutilation rather than censorship that bothered the judge. Defending their right to edit, ABC's lawyers were anxious to prove that even the BBC imposed certain standards of good taste on the Pythons.

THE JUDGE: I am not sure whether I think the BBC standards are relevant, the ABC standards are relevant or any standards are relevant. It seems to me the question is whether an author has the right to have his show put on as he produced it or not. I think that's the legal question we have to face. I am perfectly prepared to believe that ABC made some cuts in good faith to conform to standards, but I do not think that is the question I have to decide.

The only way to tell if the Pythons' work really had been mutilated was to compare the two versions, and though Clarence Fried appeared to be anxious to put the moment off, late in the morning a colour television set and a video recorder were wheeled into the court and set up facing the jury benches. The judge and the court recorder settled themselves in the jury box in front of the set, and then everyone else who could crammed in around them. Palin and Gilliam stood leaning on the jury box, ready to make their points as they went along.

THE JUDGE: Is there anything else you want to say before we get started?
PALIN: I hope you like it.

The original *Monty Python* show number 3, subtitled 'L.E. War' was shown first. ('L.E.' is a reference to the BBC's Light Entertainment department; the programme's theme was the entertainment industry's trivialization of war.) The show went down well in the informal atmosphere created by everyone sitting together in the jury box. The judge exchanged meaningful glances with the clerk over some of the jokes against court procedure, and the court recorder, who had never seen *Monty Python* before, laughed loudly. From time to time the tape was stopped so that the Pythons could make a point.

PALIN: Can we stop a minute? At the end of the dance, when they do that bit and the thing with their arms, part of ABC's cuts, in fact cut number 4, cut number 4, says, '14 seconds deleted at end of military trial sequence to delete shots of men showing backsides to camera as well as obscene arm gestures.' This is one of the things where I feel they have submitted the word – they put in the word obscene. We don't hold that is an obscene arm gesture.

The original tape was followed by the twenty-two and a half minutes that were left in the ABC version of the same episode. The Pythons felt from the atmosphere in court that their point was made. Blank spaces had been left in the tape where the commercials would appear, and the audience had to sit through them in an embarrassed silence. When the court broke for lunch at twenty past one the Pythons, who had never thought that they could take on a big corporation like ABC and win, began to hope.

The afternoon, however, was mainly ABC's, and corporations are as sensitive about their reputations as actors and writers. They had to win. There was to begin with the purely legal argument: the Pythons' copyright was only in the scripts, the actual tapes belonged to the BBC, and the BBC had passed on to Time Life Films the right to edit them in accordance with American commercial practice. Since the BBC and Time Life were not in court – except as represented by witnesses – there was no case to answer, for the Pythons' dispute was with them. The legal argument, however, also conveyed an assumption about the way things were done. The institutions assumed they had a right, even a duty, to edit the material they bought. On the witness stand Bob Shanks presented himself as a friend to writers and performers who had been on their side of the fence in his time – 'I hate to give up a word, a one liner, or anything' – indeed, in fairness he had after all decided to take a gamble with the Pythons in the first place. But his view of the relationship between corporation and comic was clear.

BOB SHANKS: There is no question that in working in American commercial television cuts are required of two kinds: one, mechanical, to fit the formats of the programmes, because we are on very tight time schedules in commercial television, and the second one, to conform with Standards and Practices' procedures which is a standard provision of all three network contracts, I believe.

ABC was backed up by representatives of the two other broadcasting institutions involved, Time Life and the BBC. The director of the BBC's office in New York, David Webster, who was very unhappy about the whole affair taking place underneath his nose when he knew almost nothing about it, was firm that BBC tapes belonged to the BBC. Asked specifically about the Python tapes he replied, 'I would assume that the BBC has the copyright and therefore could run it backwards if it wanted to.' An exchange with Time Life's Director of Programme Planning, Peter Hansen, revealed the general attitude in the television entertainment business.

FRIED: Was there any cannibalization of the programme that you saw in the cut version?

HANSEN: No, not in the accepted – industry accepted – sense of the word.

ABC's vice-president in charge of contracts, Richard Burns, summed it up when he said that if the company did not have the right to edit, it would be a total bar to the material's commercial use. ABC had a right to edit, and an obligation to censor.

BURNS: The very reason for the existence of the ABC's Department of Broadcast Standards and Practice is to exercise a responsible judgment over the programme material that ABC puts on the air, not only for the stations that it owns, which are only five in number, but for the other almost two hundred stations around the country that comprise the ABC Television network. I think that this is a central function for any broadcaster, and especially so for a network where you are exercising this judgment de facto, on behalf of two hundred broadcasters.

It is worth looking more closely at the responsible judgments ABC decided to make on behalf of the two hundred stations, and, de facto, for an audience of several million. They were deeply concerned to protect the late-night public from such profanities as 'good Lord', 'oh my God', 'hell', 'damn', and the purely descriptive word for a female dog, 'bitch', as in 'King George bitch'. Men in women's clothing worried them a great deal, and explicit homosexual or heterosexual references, though obviously meant to be funny, had to be cut out. In the light of the nightly mass slaughter on American television, ABC were strangely sensitive to *Monty Python*'s comic violence. Sex and violence came far too dangerously close together in Terry Gilliam's animations of exploding Queen Victorias and naked ladies.

The curiosity of ABC's argument was that the commercial networks and the PBS system were both governed by the same code laid down by the Federal Communications Commission. But as the judge found out from Clarence Fried, these standards 'are much more rigid as far as commercial [broadcasting] is concerned'. Fearing that they have more to lose, the commercial networks censor themselves more rigidly, but, as again the judge pointed out, PBS had not found it necessary to edit the previous *Python* shows. (Indeed, when *Monty Python* Series IV was later broadcast by PBS, there was no censorship, and no trouble with the FCC.) At no point would any executive admit that ABC's version was less funny than the original.

Beyond justifying their assumptions about their responsibilities as an institution, ABC had two further reasons for needing to win the case: they did not like being brought into court by a group of comedians, and they feared that if they lost, others would want to do the same thing. The case had to be considered in terms of the financial damage done to either side: the Pythons and the damage to their professional reputation, ABC and the damage done to theirs. Not only would the company be put to considerable expense in changing their schedules at the last minute – the *TV Guide* was already printed – Richard Burns argued that a decision against them would hurt in other ways.

BURNS: ABC would be subject to a lot of unfavourable publicity which I don't think under the circumstances would be deserved. It would create problems for us in our dealings with other distributors and other packagers. It would indicate to the people who supply programmes to us a certain sloppiness, perhaps, in our organization in that we might fail to check out the rights in the programme material that we are given. It would have other effects that I think generally could be grouped under the heading of putting us in an unfavourable light, both with the Government and with the public.

In making his final point in his case for refusing the injunction, Clarence Fried made an appeal for the consideration of what he termed the public interest.

FRIED: The public interest here is that if at zero hour writers, directors, performers, cameramen, whoever is involved in a programme is coming in and asking a court for a preliminary injunction, if programmes are taken off the air the viewing public is going to be buried in a chaotic state and the programming will be impossible.

What Fried meant by the public interest came out more clearly after the hearing, 'to accept the conditions imposed by the court would only invite actions for injunctive relief by every writer, artist, cameraman, director, performer, musician, lighting engineer, set and dress designer, editor and sound effects man and many others who contribute to making a motion picture or television programme on the claim that his component part in the composite undertaking was not according to his liking or artistic sense'. If the creators of programmes established rights of control over their material, ABC's, rather than the viewing public's life was going to be made more difficult.

Forced into court by the Pythons, ABC was made to reveal its corporate thinking. But the Pythons, removed from their customary condition of silliness, and in no position to rubbish the proceedings with their usual deflationary tactics, were forced to articulate some of their values too. They had shown that their artistic intentions had been destroyed and the programmes mutilated. They had argued, not very convincingly, that they would lose money through being presented by ABC on network television. They also showed that they were not just worried about the integrity of the work, but the work as integrity. Terry Gilliam, who knew the way American corporations worked far better than the British Pythons brought up by the benevolent BBC, put their case:

TERRY GILLIAM: I think one of the important things to me about what has happened with *Monty Python* in the States is there are a lot of people who have come to believe in *Python* as a form of honesty, I suppose, as opposed to what is normally presented on television. Here is a show that is outspoken, says what it wants to say, does extraordinary things, takes all sorts of chances, is not out to sell corn plaster, or anything; it is out to entertain, surprise, enlighten even, the people that are viewing it.

By putting out the show we are talking about, I think it is a very compromising show. I think it completely – I think it could be read, and I think the first show was read, this is my impression from people I have spoken to, things I have heard, that *Monty Python* has finally accepted the standards of commercial television as opposed to our own standards. It has always been our standards that have determined what we do and why we do it, and it seems by the popularity of the show and all the things that are going on with it, that we have been proved right to at least some people. Not everybody in the world – we never intended to impress everybody in the world.

FRIED: Your Honour, I submit this narrative is certainly beyond the purpose of his objection to the programme.

THE JUDGE: I want to hear why these people feel that they will be damaged, Mr Fried, and you can argue that some of it is not cognizable or that it is,

but I will hear it. You were saying that some people believed—

GILLIAM: I really think there is an element of integrity in what we have done. Good, bad, or indifferent, it doesn't really enter into it. It seems to me, it is an element of integrity. I think the show that is going out compromises that integrity. It is very recognizable as something we haven't done in the past, and it makes our believability totally – it brings it all into question. I think that's one of the things that's been very important to us. It's been the fun of it all, really.

I also think that in the case of the show going out in areas that haven't actually seen *Monty Python*, there has been a lot of press, there has been a lot of publicity about *Monty Python* in *Newsweek* and lots of national papers. This is the first chance for people to see it. They are going to look at this thing and say, 'So what?' That may be the end of their relationship with *Monty Python*. That may be it in a nutshell. They look at it, 'Well, what was that about?' The few people they heard say 'It is awful', 'Righto, awful.'

FRIED: This is pure speculation.

THE JUDGE: Of course it is speculation. Speculation by somebody who is as close to the subject as possible. I don't know how we can possibly tell what the damage may be without some speculation. You can bring your speculators in and I will be glad to hear them.

GILLIAM: Pure speculation. I have no figures to back me up, I have no marketing research groups to back me up. I just know in my guts that this is true.

People I have talked to, we are in touch with them, we try to be in touch with people as opposed to ending up doing a show that is produced at the top of a very tall building that is detached from most forms of reality.

At half past five Judge Lasker gathered up his papers and retired 'to consult the oracle'. He returned half an hour later with a judgment that first raised, and then dashed, the hopes of each side in turn. 'Gentlemen,' he began, 'you will have to understand that I have not had the benefit of talking to all my script writers or having this material edited one way or another, but because I know that the parties are exceedingly anxious to have a decision one way or the other so that they can either live with it or appeal immediately, and that time is of the essence, I will dictate my decision at this time . . .'

Judge Lasker began by commenting that, as he had thought at the beginning of the hearing, both parties had acted in good faith. He also commented that misunderstandings such as had occurred should be avoided by improved procedures in the industry: 'of all industries there should not be failure of communication within the communications industry'. The next part was for the Pythons:

THE JUDGE: I find that the plaintiffs have established an impairment of the integrity of their work. Though the revised version, which I have no doubt was edited by those concerned with care and a desire to preserve the original quality of the work, does breathe the originality and fantasy and comedy of the uncut version, it nevertheless has caused the film or programme in my view to lose its iconoclastic verve.

He further commented that the cuts were heavy, 'twenty-two minutes out of ninety minutes, which comes near the border at which one might say that the cuts, if not fatal, certainly made it very difficult for the patient to live in good health'.

Before the Pythons could congratulate themselves, however, came the bad news. He refused to grant an injunction because of the confusion over who owned the copyright in the shows, and the question of whether or not the BBC and Time Life should be parties in the action. His main reason, however, was that ABC would lose money if the injunction were granted, and even though they might be able to recover that from Time Life or the BBC, their reputation in the industry would be irreparably damaged. Lasker also felt that the Pythons had shown 'a somewhat disturbing casualness' in their approach to the problem before first seeing ABC's version in November, and so had precipitated the present rush.

ABC's victory, was not total, for Lasker said that he would accept an application from the Pythons for some sort of disclaimer to be shown at the beginning of the show when ABC transmitted it, to indicate their attitude to the changes that had been made. He was ready to hear that application now, but as the precise wording had to be worked out, it was agreed that the lawyers would meet and get the matter agreed on the following Monday morning. The hearing ended at 6.15.

The Pythons stayed behind briefly to work out the wording of a disclaimer with their lawyers – Terry Gilliam recalls being asked by an ABC executive if it would be possible to make it funny. While they were still there the clerk of the court told them that Judge Lasker had asked for a private word, and they went to shake his hand, for Lasker wanted to confirm that he was a fan. Later still, in the freezing cold of a cab-less Foley Square, they encountered the judge again on his way home, and there was a bizarre scene at the subway station, as the helpful judge passed the Pythons subway tokens through the forbidding iron bars of the subway entrance grill. Together they travelled to Grand Central Station. Later that night Palin and Gilliam flew back to London. Years later they learned that the judge's childhood nickname had been – Monty.

The story, however, by no means ends there, for the Pythons still had a $1,000,000 suit against ABC, and they had only lost a preliminary injunction, not the case. The next round again went to ABC, for on the following Monday, after Judge Lasker ordered them to show a modified version of the Pythons' disclaimer:

> 1. This text shall be shown by a constant image for the duration of ~~one minute~~ *twenty* 20 *seconds* with a voice over reading of the text, ~~by an announcer selected by plaintiffs:~~ "The members of Monty Python wish to ~~totally~~ disassociate themselves from this program which is a compilation of their shows ~~censored and~~ edited by ABC *without their approval* ~~against their wishes and without their consent.~~"

ABC went straight to the Appeal Court, and won a stay of execution.

On 26 December when ABC's *Wide World of Entertainment* was transmitted the only indication that the Python shows were not as intended was the brief message on the screen, 'Edited for television by ABC.'

The next stage was for the Pythons to appeal against Judge Lasker's denial of a preliminary injunction. ABC were now fully alerted to the implications of the Python case, and in a letter of 2 February 1976 Robert Osterberg warned the Pythons that ABC would 'view this action as a major challenge to their censorship authority' and fight the case all the way to the United States Supreme Court if necessary. For their part the Pythons were worried about the legal expenses they were incurring, but their lawyers, feeling a commitment to the Pythons and their cause, were ready to press on to an appeal against the refusal of an injunction as part of their original fee.

Appeals of this kind do not have any of the drama, or comedy, of hearings in court. Both sides prepare the equivalent of a short paperback on the facts and legal precedents of their case, and are given a strictly limited time for oral argument. The three appeal judges then go away and think things over, maybe for months. After a series of delays the Pythons' appeal was argued on 13 April 1976, and decided on 30 June. More than six months after they had first tried to stop ABC, they got their injunction.

The decision of the United States Court of Appeals for the Second Circuit in favour of *Monty Python* is an important addition to the small body of case-law concerning the relationships of artists and their patrons. Since the second ABC show had now gone out, the appeal judges were in a different position to Judge Lasker, for no repeats were scheduled, making an injunction no longer financially harmful to ABC. They were therefore able to consider whether the case itself would succeed on its merits. They agreed with Judge Lasker that the cuts, which they calculated as twenty-seven per cent of the original material, were substantial, but they had made their minds up about the issue of copyright, about which Judge Lasker had been doubtful. The BBC might own the copyright in the video-tapes involved, but the tapes were derived from the writers' scripts, and there the copyright was certainly the Pythons'. Moreover, the Pythons' agreement with the BBC limited the BBC's entitlement to edit, and therefore the BBC had no right to pass on to Time Life Films (and so ABC) a right to edit it did not itself possess. The fact that the Pythons knew, or should have realized, that transmission on commercial television involved editing, was not a valid answer.

In deciding the question of ABC's assumed right to edit, the appeal judges had to consider the question of censorship. As they put it: 'According to the network, appellants should have anticipated that most of the excised material contained scatological references inappropriate for American television and that these scenes would be replaced with commercials, which presumably are more palatable to the American public.' They revealed that they too had made a comparison of the two versions, and it is clear that the comparison helped them to make up their minds. The judgment read:

> Several of the deletions made for ABC, such as elimination of the words 'hell' and 'damn', seem inexplicable given today's standard television fare. If, however, ABC honestly determined that the programmes were obscene in substantial part, it could have decided not to broadcast the specials at all, or it could have attempted to reconcile its differences with appellants. The network could not, however, free from a claim of infringement, broadcast in a substantially altered form a programme incorporating the script over which the group had retained control.
>
> Our resolution of these technical arguments serves to reinforce our initial inclination that the copyright law should be used to recognize the important role of the artist in our society and the need to encourage production and dissemination of artistic works by providing adequate legal protection for one who submits his work to the public. See Mazer v. Stein, 347 U.S. 201 (1954). We therefore conclude that there is a substantial likelihood that, after a full trial, appellants will succeed in proving infringement of their copyright by ABC's broadcast of edited versions of *Monty Python* programmes.

The appeal judges however, in saying that the copyright law 'should be used to recognize the important role of the artist in our society' went a stage further, and considered the question of whether the Pythons' work had been mutilated, regardless of whether ABC had a right to edit or not. American law does not recognize what in Europe is known as the *droit moral*, the moral right of the creator to have his work in the form in which he intended it. (Though Terry Gilliam did not know it, his speech in defence of the integrity of Pythons' work was an argument serving the idea of a *droit moral*.) American law recognizes financial rights, not moral rights, but the appeal judges felt nonetheless there was a chance that a full hearing would show that the mutilation of their work was financially damaging. It might also show that the mutilation was such that to call the resulting programme 'Monty Python' might be a misdescription under the Lanham Act. Finally, the appeal judges decided that the Pythons had not been dilatory in bringing their action. In the light of the possibility that it might succeed, the judges gave the Pythons an injunction as the first step towards making their case.

Whether or not the Pythons' case really would have succeeded we shall never know, for faced with the prospect of ever-escalating legal costs, both sides came to an agreement. ABC were ready to go as far as the Supreme Court if necessary in defence of their interests. The Pythons felt that they had made their point with the fans, and although the final result of their appeal received little publicity, they had established a precedent in American copyright law. ABC, now represented by their insurers' lawyers, could probably, if the case went against them, recover their losses from Time Life and the BBC, both of whom were anxious to keep out of the case. The deal, therefore, was done with Time Life and the BBC, and again it meant Python was breaking new ground in its relations with broadcasting institutions.

In return for dropping their action against ABC, and releasing the money from ABC held by their agents as payment for repeats that could not take place, Python would receive $35,000 from Time Life Films towards their court costs. More important, as far as the Pythons were concerned, as the options on the four series of *Monty Python* expired, the rights to distribute them would be returned by Time Life and the BBC, so that after 31 December 1980 the Pythons would have total control over their television work. They undertook not to broadcast the programmes in the United Kingdom, but the BBC had to deliver to them copies of all forty-five episodes of *Monty Python* that they had made. The two ABC compilations made by Time Life Films were also to be delivered to the Pythons.

The agreement was finally signed on 1 March 1979. This time the Pythons made sure that while they were still being distributed by the BBC or Time Life, the programmes would be shown in their entirety.

The ABC case was important because it revealed the workings of a huge corporation, and it showed that it was possible to take it on and win. In the process the Pythons established new rights for artists to protect their work from mutilation, and although ABC were not party to the final settlement, the corporations had been warned that it was no longer possible to pass off the re-edited and censored work of writers as the real thing.

Having made a contribution to the new laws of the entertainment industry, however, the Pythons proceeded almost immediately to run into an ancient law of the church.

11. (a) The parties hereby agree that it is of the essence of this Agreement that TLF will not cut, edit, add to, compile, interrupt for the insertion of commercials or otherwise modify the Monty Python Shows, and that TLF will specify in all agreements with its licensees and subdistributors that:

(i) they may not cut, edit, add to, compile interrupt for the insertion of commercials, or otherwise modify the Monty Python Shows;

(ii) they will show the Monty Python Shows in the form these shows are delivered to them;

(iii) in the event a licensee or subdistributor violates the terms and provisions of this paragraph 11, their license will automatically terminate and this will be without prejudice to any other rights or remedies available; and

The Stoning Place. An OFFICIAL stands there,
with some helpers, confronting the potential
stonee, MATTHIAS. A large crowd watches.
90% are women in beards. Around the
perimeter are a few Roman troops.

JEWISH OFFICIAL
Matthias son of Deuteronomy of Gath...

MATTHIAS (to Official's Helper)
Do I say yes?

OFFICIAL'S HELPER
Yes.

MATTHIAS
Yes.

OFFICIAL
You have been found guilty by the elders of the
town of uttering the name of our Lord and so as
a blasphemer you are to be stoned to death.

MATTHIAS
Look, I'd had a lovely supper and all I said to
my wife was, 'That piece of halibut was good
enough for Jehovah.'

OFFICIAL
Blasphemy! He's done it again.

WOMEN
Yes, he did.

OFFICIAL
Did you hear him?

WOMEN
Yes we did. Really.

OFFICIAL
Are there any women here today?

    The WOMEN all shake their heads. The
    OFFICIAL faces Matthias again.

OFFICIAL
Very well, by virtue of the authority vested in
me...

    One of the WOMEN throws a stone and it hits
    MATTHIAS on the knee.

MATTHIAS
Ow. Lay off. We haven't started yet.

OFFICIAL (turning around)
Come on, who threw that?

    Silence.

Who threw that stone? Come on.

    Some of the WOMEN point to the culprit.

WOMEN
She did.

He did.

He.

Him.

    During this they keep their voices as low
    as they can, in pitch but not in volume.

CULPRIT (very deep voice)
Sorry, I thought we'd started.

OFFICIAL
Go to the back.

CULPRIT (disappointed)
Oh dear.   (goes to back)

OFFICIAL
There's always one, isn't there? Now, where

Council censors to think again over a film they ban

By JOHN HUTSON

...g of Life of Brian

...ban on

R intense public pressure
...roversial new Mont...
...rian' Thanet C...
and ar...

Chip shop ban

anti-Brian Tories

THANET Council face a massive backlash of public opinion follow...
...cision to ban the new Monty Python film 'The Life o...

Auschwitz next?

Parents who have read anything about the film, "Life
Brian" will be horrified at the possibility of their
ild being allowed to see the film here in Cornwall.
The film is a cruel mockery of the religious feelings
both Christians and Jews, and so offensive in language
d presentation as to be a possible incitement to is-
lence.
The National Festival of Light reports that par...
ipt of the film, and accounts obtained from...
tes, show the film to be littered...
ter words, with the central ch...
om he has intercourse...
d the Virgin Mary...
icted by a m...
Even if...
n...

COUNCIL COULD FACE HIGH COURT ACTION

Cinema chiefs at the C...
ton made scathing comm...
about the ban which foll...
a 34-name protest ge...
from the Salem
Church in Broadstairs
Mike Vickers said:
people write to say the
like fair-haired...

Film-ban theory over rampa...

UPS OF Mods and Rockers who
t on the rampage at Milford Haven on
urday evening may have been angry
a ban on the film Life of Brian from
cal cinemas.
...is one theory being considered by police at
...who spent yesterday investigating a
...which included an attack on a
...being stolen, windows
...te of sign daubing on
...a short
...the

teenage gangs, and the head of the town's police
force, Chief-Inspector Brian Bebb, criticised parents
for not controlling their children.
He said, "It is one of the worst nights of crime we
have had for a long time, and is the work of
youngsters.
"It's about time parents' got a grip on their
children as they seem to be running wild, they
particularly on a Saturday evening. We know they
are getting cans of beer from somewhere, and
drinking them in toilets."
Presell District Council's decision to ban the
Monty Python film could have been partially
responsible, as several of the signs sprayed with
paint on buildings declared, "Brian lives on."
Milford Haven's Town Hall, a local supermarket,
...h meeting place and Hakin bridge and the
...places selected for graffiti and the council.
...and obscenities about the council.
...late on Saturday evening.

So far official repor...
at a butcher's sho...
main street. It is...
from amusement...
Several win...
large plateglass...
shop. Two va...
abandoned a...
other was re...
away.
Two da...
break into...
also the w...
Sever...
town on S...
them ar...
The
Christ...
of swe...
been...
some...

Currer...
packed
is due
of course, it
...vince...
this
Thanet ratepayers
Brian legal

V

'This sick enterprise'

Nationwide Festival of Light

The decision to sue ABC TV is a measure of the confidence the Pythons gained between 1969 and 1975. The 'period in the wilderness' after making *Monty Python* series IV and *The Holy Grail* gave the team the space they needed to follow up their individual interests: Terry Gilliam directed *Jabberwocky*; Michael Palin starred in the BBC's *Ripping Yarns*, with a Palin/Jones script; Terry Jones wrote his book *Chaucer's Knight*; Graham Chapman moved into film production with *The Odd Job*; Eric Idle founded *Rutland Weekend Television*; and John Cleese created *Fawlty Towers*. These individual projects were a relief from the ruthless mutual criticism of the group and an opportunity to prove that you could do some of the things that did not come your way in the normal division of labour within the team. There was (and is) always a question as to whether all six would ever work together again, yet *Monty Python* continued to exist, both as an image in the mind of the public and as a financial identity, particularly as the profits from *The Holy Grail* proved unexpectedly large.

If the six were to work together again, it would almost certainly be on another film. *The Holy Grail* brought this about, for when it was released in Europe early in 1976, more than a year after it was completed, the Pythons came together again to promote the film. Refreshed by their absence from each other, the Pythons found they had plenty of time to enjoy each other's company again, sitting around in restaurants

and airport lounges. The idea for a new film had been in the air ever since the party in New York to launch *The Holy Grail* in the spring of 1975. Asked what their next project would be, Eric Idle quipped, *'Jesus Christ: Lust for Glory.'* It was a joke, but the joke stuck, and came up again one evening in a bar in Amsterdam in February 1976. The idea that Jesus was a carpenter and ended up nailed to a wooden cross appealed to Terry Gilliam's macabre sense of humour, and some awful jokes were made. A few days later, at a Chinese restaurant in Gerrard Street, London, the group decided that they might be on to something. Eric Idle has written in an unpublished essay:

> Here were some of the basic thoughts and impulses of Western society, which had been inculcated into everyone and yet no one was allowed to refer to them or deal with them unless they were part of a religious body or organization which was dedicated to the promulgation of the very things we wanted to examine. We were drawn to the fact that this area was indeed taboo for all kinds of comedy.

The Python method was well at work. Typically, they had chosen precisely the wrong moment to set it in operation.

```
                    SEQUENCE OF SKETCHES

    1. THE SCHOOL         a) All Things Bright & Beautiful
                          b) Rugger Match
                          c) Funeral Service
                          d) Sherry
                          e) Scripture

    2. THE NATIVITY       a) The Shepherds
                          b) Three Wise Men
                          c) The Inn
                          d) Manger Scene
                          e) School Nativity

    3. BRIAN'S YOUTH      a) Romanes Eunt Domus
                          b) Terry of Nazareth
                          c) Lots more about Terry Of Nazareth

    4. TO CAPERNAUM       a) Brian and Wendy
                          b) Stoning
                          c) Sermon on the Mount
                          d) Big Nose
                          e) Pub
                          f) Magistrate's House
                          g) Amphitheatre
                          h) Brian and the Resistance

    5. TO JERUSALEM       a) Otto
                          b) Leper and Psychopath
                          c) Healed Looney
                          d) Chicken Stall
                          e) The Extras
                          f) Fleeing the Romans
                          g) Boring and Blood & Thunder Prophets
                          h) Brian Teaches
                          i) Matthew Levi's Crucifixion
                          j) Slapstick, French Film, Matthias House
                          k) The Street, Shepherds & Simon

    6. RETURN TO NAZARETH a) Cheryl and Karen
                          b) Brian's Parentage
                          c) Hampstead Lady
                          d) After Brian's Performance

    7. TO JERUSALEM       a) Sibling Judith
                          b) Annas and Caiaphas
                          c) Brian and Ben
                          d) Brian's Crucifixion

    8. SCHOOL             a) Reading "The Martyrdom of St. Brian"
```

```
BRIAN:      Yes..I,like you,hate the Romans and all things Roman.

2ND. R:     Well.."hate"'s putting it a bit strongly...

3RD.R :     Yes..I wouldn't say we "hated" them. It's a bit of a sweeping generalisation.

R.LEADER:   Well we do hate them don't we ?

2nd. R:     Well we don't like them,certainly.

R.LEADER:   That's what I mean.

2ND. R:     We..ll..it's not quite the same. "Not liking" somebody is not the same as
            positively hating somebody. I mean,I might possibly"like" some
            individual Romans...

3RD.R :     Is"like" the right word ? I think its more."admire"...

2ND R:      Admire,yes.
```

```
3RD R:      I admire some of the things they've done...

            VOICE FROM THE BACK

VOICE:      The aqueduct !

2ND R:      Yes..the aqueduct's a good example.

R.LEADER:   (A LITTLE RELUCTANTLY) Yes.. yes..the aqueduct,I suppose,is one good thing ..

VOICE:      And the sanitation !

3RD R:      Oh yes..sanitation. You remember what the city used to be like

VOICE:      Couldn't have done that without the aqueduct !

            MURMURS OF AGREEMENT

R.LEADER:   Alright,I'll grant you that the aqueduct and the sanitation are two
            first class things that the Romans have done..
```

After a summer spent on individual projects, holidays and research, the first writing-meeting for the Pythons' new film was held in December 1976. Meanwhile on 2 November 1976, Mrs Mary Whitehouse had received a copy of the 3–16 June edition of the homosexual newspaper, *Gay News*. Her attention was drawn to a poem by James Kirkup, 'The Love That Dares To Speak Its Name', a fanciful description of homosexual activity between a Roman Centurion and the crucified Jesus Christ. On 12 November Mrs Whitehouse decided to bring a private prosecution against *Gay News* on the grounds of blasphemy, and the Director of Public Prosecutions gave her permission to go ahead. On 20 December the need for preliminary committal proceedings to be heard in a magistrates's court was avoided by a judge granting a voluntary bill of indictment, and the case was sent for trial on a charge of blasphemous libel to the Old Bailey.

Mrs Whitehouse was already something of an expert on the laws of blasphemy. In 1972 she had tried to bring a prosecution against the BBC for transmitting an episode of Johny Speight's *Till Death Us Do Part*, in which Alf Garnett was disparaging on the subject of the virgin birth, but the Director of Public Prosecutions decided that the case was unlikely to be successful because of the constitutional position of the BBC. In April 1976 the National Viewers' and Listeners' Association were alarmed to discover that the Swedish film-maker, Jens Jorgen Thorsen, was planning to come to England with a view to making *The Many Faces of Jesus Christ*, a film which reportedly was to feature Jesus in various and vigorous forms of sexual activity. While seeking further advice about blasphemy, Mrs Whitehouse wrote to the Home Secretary, Roy Jenkins, and asked him to declare Thorsen an undesirable alien. Jenkins refused, but National VALA launched a fierce campaign, and in September both Cardinal Hulme and the Archbishop of Canterbury joined in the protests against Thorsen. In the meantime James Callaghan succeeded Harold Wilson as Prime Minister, and Mr Callaghan let it be known that Jens Jorgen Thorsen would indeed be unwelcome in Britain. To date, *The Many Faces of Jesus Christ* has yet to be made.

The *Gay News* prosecution grew out of the Thorsen campaign, for, as Mrs Whitehouse wrote to her lawyer

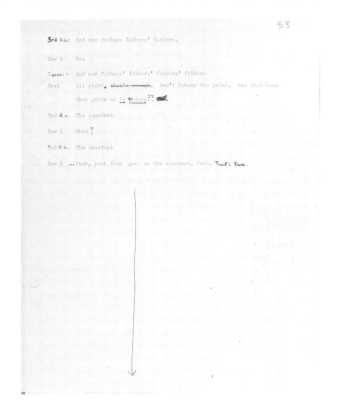

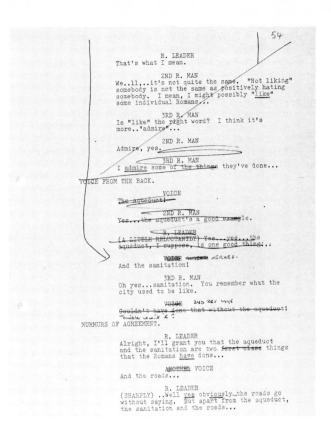

in November 1976, a successful action 'would kill the Thorsen film stone dead – and a great deal more.' What that great deal more was, she did not specify. The criminal charge of blasphemous libel was brought against *Gay News* Ltd and the paper's editor, Denis Lemon. Their crime was to have published James Kirkup's poem and the illustration that went with it. A charge against the printers of *Gay News* was dropped and it was decided not to prosecute James Kirkup because he was legally within his rights in writing the poem, even though *Gay News* was not within its rights in publishing it.

When the case came up for trial at the Old Bailey on 4 July 1977 fifty-five years had elapsed since the last successful prosecution for blasphemous libel, although as recently as 1971 a private action brought by Lady Birdwood against the play *The Council of Love* had failed on a technicality. And as the presiding judge, Mr Justice King-Hamilton, reminded the jury, the law was still the law, whether it had been recently used or not. In earlier centuries, he explained, it was regarded as blasphemous simply to deny the existence of God, but this restriction on free thinking was gradually relaxed, provided that the denial was made in a decent and sober manner. 'But what was still regarded as blasphemy, as it had been in all the earlier cases and still is regarded today,' the judge told the jury in his summing-up, 'was an element of irreverence, scurrility, profanity, vilification or licentious abuse coupled with the Christian religion, or any sacred person, or any sacred object.' It was the duty of the jury to decide whether the poem in *Gay News* fell into this category as a blasphemous libel.

A charge of blasphemous libel is far more serious than an ordinary charge of libel brought in the civil courts because it falls in the category of criminal libel. An ordinary libel is a published statement that is calculated to bring someone into public ridicule or damage his reputation. It is a civil offence and the usual remedy is the payment of damages. A criminal libel, however, makes one liable to a prison sentence, for it is a libel so outrageous or offensive that the angry feelings that it arouses might lead to a breach of the peace (technically, that is to say, it might lead to violence). A blasphemous libel is a criminal libel where the object of ridicule is not an individual but the Christian religion,

15 Continued

　　　　　　　ALL
No blackmail!!!!

　　　　　　　REG
Right. They've bled us white the
bastards. They've taken everything
we had, not just from us, from our
fathers and from our fathers' fathers.

　　　　　　　STAN
And our fathers' fathers' fathers.

　　　　　　　REG
Yes.

　　　　　　　STAN
And our fathers' fathers' fathers'
fathers.

　　　　　　　REG
All right. Don't labour the point,
Stan. And what have they given us
in return?

They pause smugly.

Voice from masked commando.

　　　　　　　XERXES
The aqueduct.

　　　　　　　REG
What?

　　　　　　　XERXES
The aqueduct.

　　　　　　　REG
... Yeah, yeah they gave us the
aqueduct. Yeah. That's true.

　　　　　　　MASKED COMMANDO
And the sanitation!

　　　　　　　STAN
Oh yes ... sanitation. You remember
what the city used to be like, Reg.

Murmurs of agreement.

　　　　　　　REG
Alright, I'll grant you that the
aqueduct and the sanitation are two
things that the Romans have done ...

and the law is so framed that the publisher's intention is irrelevant. It does not matter whether the publisher actually intended to blaspheme; it is simply enough to publish the offending material.

In the circumstances, since Kirkup's poem depicted Christ as the active and passive participant in acts of sodomy and oral sex, the eloquence of Denis Lemon's defence lawyer, John Mortimer, could do little. On 12 July the Jury decided by a majority verdict of ten to two that the publication *was* a blasphemous libel. Judge King-Hamilton sentenced Lemon to nine months in prison, but suspended the sentence for eighteen months (thus he would go to prison if he did it again) and fined him £500. *Gay News* Ltd was fined £1,000 and the costs of the case were awarded against the defendants. As the instigator of this private prosecution, Mrs Whitehouse had won a victory, though the defence immediately entered an appeal.

The *Gay News* trial brought forth a great deal of righteous indignation on both sides. During the months before the trial *Gay News* accumulated a fighting fund of £20,000, to which Python contributed. Graham Chapman felt particularly involved, for he was one of the people who had put up the money to launch *Gay News* in the first place. Chapman and Jones also gave support to the hurriedly formed Free Speech Movement, which reprinted James Kirkup's poem, along with the members' names and its address, with the deliberate intention of inviting prosecution. The fact that Mrs Whitehouse did *not* prosecute the Free Speech Movement was taken as an indication that her real intention all along was to prosecute a newspaper for homosexuals and not the blasphemy itself. Mrs Whitehouse's own news-sheet, the *Viewer and Listener*, which she edited (and, judging from the prose style, probably also wrote) gave this version of events in its October 1977 issue:

Immediately the trial was over the homosexual/humanist/intellectual lobby launched itself into action, concentrating primarily upon the correspondence columns of *The Times*, but using every national and provincial paper. Quite a spectacle!

The strategy of the lobby became abundantly clear – and immediately. It was to smother the issue of blasphemy by the constant repetition of the theme that the real purpose of the trial had been to persecute a minority – namely homosexuals.

It would seem that people of Mrs Whitehouse's persuasion have no particular fondness for homosexuals – a 1975 Festival of Light pamphlet, *The Truth in Love: the Christian and the homosexual* (note the capitalization) says that the acceptance of homosexuality by any community is 'the mark of a society which is decadent and under judgment' – and the public reaction to the trial showed that many people believed that homosexuality was the real issue. But as a result, the *Gay News* prosecution proved counter-productive. Mrs

Whitehouse had successfully revived an ancient law in defence of the Christian religion, but in the process James Kirkup's poem had become widely known and widely circulated through the Free Speech Movement. On the other hand, public reaction to the trial left her, in her own words to interviewers Michael Tracey and David Morrison, 'dreadfully isolated'. It may be that the public's interpretation of Mrs Whitehouse's role in the *Gay News* affair affected her policy towards later events.

On the other hand, those wishing to treat lightly of any aspect of the Christian religion now knew that they had the law looking closely over their shoulder.

The first draft of the Pythons' new film was completed in July 1977, the same month that the *Gay News* trial took place. The subject of *Jesus Christ: Lust for Glory* had altered, not because of the Whitehouse prosecution, but because trial scripts had shown that it wasn't funny. When it came to the writing-meetings, it turned out that nobody had written anything about Christ, but a great deal of the goings-on around him – the followers, the chroniclers, the churches – came in for criticism. A reading of the Gospels and their conflicting accounts of the life of Christ threw up the idea that there might have been a thirteenth disciple, Brian, and *The Gospel According to St Brian* was toyed with. Brian began to take over and the next stage was *Brian of Nazareth*, a parallel story to that of Christ, before they finally settled on *Monty Python's Life of Brian*. Aware that they were in a delicate area, they informally sought the opinion of a Canon of St George's, Windsor Castle, who read the script and listened to a tape they had made of the dialogue. The Canon's letter seemed reassuring. At the beginning of 1978 the Pythons took

Dec. 5th 1977.

THE CLOISTERS
WINDSOR CASTLE
SL4 1NJ

Dear Graham
    I'm sorry to have kept your script so long. There has been no time for reading it through in the last few days
    It seems clear to me that the script is not meant to be blasphemous and that it is extracting the maximum comedy out of false religion and religious illusions and out of all whose religion as a cover for their particular form of sin.
    But having said that, I remain fairly sure that it would prove extremely offensive to a great many Christians and Jews. Those who react to first impressions will think you are mocking at Christ and those who think about it afterwards will feel that you have set up the whole area of the life of Jesus as a crazy

the advice of their tax accountants and flew off to complete a screenplay in the creative surroundings of Heron Bay, Barbados.

The Pythons had made the deliberate decision not to look for a backer for the project until they had what they thought was a solid screenplay. 'Finding money isn't the hard part,' Eric Idle has said, 'it's writing a good script in the first place.' The trip to Barbados shows the Pythons' faith in their powers, for the sets, crowds, costumes and location filming demanded for even a miniaturized Biblical epic would need at least £2 million. Barbados is a favourite wintering-place for Eric Idle, and just before the others arrived to join him, he met Barry Spikings, the managing director of Britain's leading film production company, EMI, who was in Barbados for a Christmas holiday. They talked about the film, and Idle teased Spikings by saying that this wasn't 'an EMI film'. That whetted Spikings's appetite, and on 19 January 1978, while the Pythons were still working on their final draft in Barbados, Spikings telephoned the man the Pythons had chosen to produce the film, John Goldstone. (Goldstone had been executive producer for *The Holy Grail*.) The contact with EMI was propitious. The company had distributed *The Holy Grail* in the United Kingdom (though they had refused to finance it) and, under the joint managing directorship of Barry Spikings and Michael Deeley, had put fresh aggression into its film-making operations with ambitious projects, like *The Deer Hunter*, that competed with the Americans on their own ground in Hollywood. A British written, directed and performed film, produced by a major British company, was a psychological boost that the home industry badly needed and, after being shown a script, Barry Spikings was enthusiastic about making a deal.

On 28 January Barry Spikings and Michael Deeley were quoted in *Screen International*: 'It is our firm belief that EMI will emerge as one of the world's biggest producing and distributing organizations in 1978.' On the same day John Goldstone went to Spikings's home and spent three hours discussing the film. Spikings had cleared the project with the board of EMI, and he agreed a budget of £2 million. When the bronzed Pythons returned from Barbados later that weekend Goldstone was able to tell them that it looked as though they had an agreement.

Setting up a film is a complex business. There has to be elaborate planning of the physical aspects of production, and there are elaborate arrangements to be made before the contract is actually signed. Terry Jones and Terry Gilliam hurried off to look at locations in Tunisia, props began to be assembled and the costume designers flew to Rome to hire suitable Biblical-epic wardrobes. Being a Moslem country, Tunisia was thought a less provocative location than Roman Catholic Italy or Spain or, for that matter, twentieth-century Palestine. There was the added convenience that Franco Zeffirelli had left behind a number of sets

built for the TV film spectacular, *Jesus of Nazareth*. Filming was scheduled to begin in April.

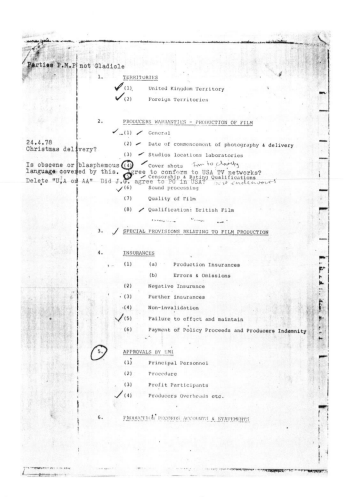

Back in London, John Goldstone and EMI were working out their contractual arrangements. The Pythons were anxious that they, and not EMI, should have control over the final shape of the film, something EMI said it had never conceded before, though it was understood that this was a special case. If EMI agreed to the Pythons' terms for artistic control, then the only editing forced upon them would be from the need to get a suitable certificate. Confident that they would secure a contract, the Pythons allowed pre-production costs to mount, although negotiations were delayed by Barry Spikings's necessary absence in America. Time was getting short, with filming soon to begin, when a final meeting was arranged for 28 February. (On 21 February the *Gay News* case went before the Court of Appeal. On 23 February in the House of Lords Ted Willis failed to get a second reading for his bill repealing the common law offence of blasphemy.) On the day before the meeting, John Goldstone summed up the state of play:

```
1.) Blasphemy (see copy letter)
    If this comes up in their script approval provision I think
    we should agree to be prepared to at least have some cover
    shots on this sequence so that if there are any problems at
    a later date we are suitably prepared.  The question of
    blasphemy is a legal point in any event and is subject to
    interpretation out of either our or EMI's control.

2.) Censorship
    It was my understanding that as long as we got a censor
    certificate this would be acceptable, although in fact to have
the film 'X' rated particularly in the USA wouldnot seem to reflect
    our intentionto have the film seen by as wide an audience as
    possible.  In the draft contract EMI are virtually insisting

                                                Contd/...
```

```
Continuation

2) (Contd) that the film gets no more than an 'AA' in the UK and
           'PG' in the USA.   In any event the equivalent of an
           'AA' is 'R' not 'PG'.  Both 'AA' and 'R' are one
           step up from the certificate we had on the Holy Grail.

3)         Cutting Rights
           The wording in the draft contract (extract attached)
           is in any event not practical, I have already expressed
           my views which have been passed on to EMI as follows:-

           "It is our intention to do an intermediate dub of the
           film to ascertain half way through the post production
           period whether the cut of the film that we have is
           working.  We should at this point let EMI see the film
           and listen to any suggestions they might have and
           consider them accordingly but without any obligation to
           accept them.  We will then proceed to getting a final
           cut and dub, have the negative cut, make a CRI protection
           and at that point preview the film.  It must be fully
           realized without shame or embarrassment that it has
           been in the past and is again normal practice to try out
           a film on the general public who are better judges of
           whether or not a film is working, in particular with
           comedy: Woody Allen and Mel Brooks try their films out
           very thoroughly before finalising.  The comparison to
           these two gentlemen is important because they also have
           an original and personal type of comedy which no one
                    advise them on.  If after previews in the UK
                    not totally satisfactory then changes
                    d the film should again '
                    on knows h
```

The meeting with Barry Spikings was much briefer than expected. Spikings began by raising a whole series of difficulties in the proposed contract, but Goldstone cut him short by asking him straight-forwardly if EMI accepted the Pythons' screenplay as written, for they were not prepared to make any changes. Straightforwardly, but with considerable embarrassment, Spikings gave the answer no. The deal was off.

It was not Barry Spikings's decision to cancel the project, but that of EMI's sixty-nine-year-old chief executive, Lord Delfont. While Spikings was in America during February the chief executive's attention had been drawn to the contents of the *Brian* script. Lord Delfont's taste in entertainment was formed in an earlier era than that of *Monty Python*, and he decided that whereas his brother, Lord Grade, had done very well out of *Jesus of Nazareth*, he would be in an embarrassing position with *The Life of Brian*. The reason given officially for dropping the project was the high cost of the film and the Pythons' demand for artistic control, but as *Screen International* commented: 'It seemed though that Lord Delfont was more concerned by what he considered were the "blasphemous" aspects of the script; indeed, even "anti-semitism".' Though *Brian* was innocent of both these charges and proved highly profitable, Lord Delfont has remained unrepentant:

> I ... believe that there are some subjects not to make – however talented the film makers. I refused to finance *The Life of Brian*. I make no apologies although this is now a success at the box office. That was my decision because it was not a film I wanted my company's money to be invested in. I would not show a film excusing Hitler at our cinemas. I refused to show a play critical of Churchill at one of our theatres. If others subsequently went on to profit from my withdrawal – so be it.

In March 1978 the Pythons cancelled their plans to start filming in Tunisia in April. In the same month the Court of Appeal confirmed the fines on Denis Lemon and *Gay News* Ltd, but set aside the prison sentence – and EMI announced a huge slump in profits.

Lord Delfont's personal act of censorship could have cost *The Life of Brian* its existence; as it turned out, a remarkable personal act of patronage meant that all it cost was six months' delay (though even that affected the profitability of the film). It gets too hot to film in Tunisia after April, so, with costumes hired, crews booked and sets half-built, filming was postponed until September – with the hope that £2 million could be raised from somewhere. The Pythons had already spent the equivalent of the entire budget of *And Now For Something Completely Different*, and started legal proceedings against EMI to try to recover some of the money lost. EMI settled out of court.

Eric Idle and John Goldstone flew to New York to talk to people who might put up the money, a humiliating business that got them nowhere. Throughout this time Idle was in contact with ex-Beatle George Harrison. Harrison was an ardent Python fan. He and Idle had first met at the première of *The Holy Grail* in Los Angeles and were thrown out of the projection booth where they were having a quiet chat. Harrison made a guest appearance in *Rutland Weekend Television* and

played a small part in Idle's Beatles' spoof, *The Rutles*, broadcast that March. Harrison kept assuring Eric Idle: 'I'll get you the money. You want the money, I'll give you the money.' This is an old showbiz joke and Idle did not take him seriously for he did not believe that even an ex-Beatle could personally raise – or risk – £2 million.

Having failed to raise funds in New York, Idle and Goldstone flew to Hollywood, and it was there that they learned that George Harrison *had* got them the money. He and his business manager, Denis O'Brien, were ready to go ahead. As John Cleese said later, George Harrison put up the money 'apparently for no more reason than that he wanted to see the film.'

With George Harrison and Denis O'Brien as executive producers, *Monty Python's Life of Brian* was shot in September and October 1978, directed by Terry Jones and designed by Terry Gilliam, with everyone acting and contributing their criticism. Surrounded by a happy band of Moslems, the Pythons concentrated on getting the film made, but the threat of a prosecution for blasphemy would not go away. In May 1978 Denis Lemon and *Gay News* Ltd had been given leave to take their appeal to the very highest court, the Appeal Judges in the House of Lords. The arguments were presented between 20 and 27 November 1978. Judgment was given on 21 February 1979, just as John Goldstone was beginning the delicate task of negotiations with the British film censors. (All along, the worry was about British rather than American censorship, for the American constitution guarantees freedom of expression, even of blasphemous opinions.)

Of the five Law Lords who heard the final *Gay News* appeal, Viscount Dilhorne, Lord Russell of Killowen and Lord Scarman upheld the conviction, Lord Diplock and Lord Edmund Davies dissented. The conviction therefore stood, making it clear beyond any doubt that it was no defence against a charge of blasphemy to say that you did not intend to blaspheme. Ever since their idea was first conceived the Pythons had argued that they had funny, not blasphemous intentions, but that would be no protection if a charge were brought. Moreover, Lord Scarman's judgment in particular seemed actually to extend the area covered by the laws of blasphemy. His judgment began with the comment that, far from the offence of blasphemous libel serving no useful purpose: 'I think there is a case for legislation extending it to protect the religious beliefs and feelings of non-Christians. The offence belongs in a group of criminal offences designed to safeguard the internal tranquillity of the kingdom.' The law of blasphemy, Lord Scarman argued, imposed a continuing 'duty on all of us to refrain from insulting or outraging the religious feelings of others.' In view of the known feelings of such organizations as the Festival of Light, the Pythons were certainly in danger of a brush with the law.

It is now generally agreed that *Monty Python's Life of*

Brian may be outrageous, but it is not blasphemous. As they completed the script, the Pythons worked further and further away from *Jesus Christ: Lust for Glory* and built in scenes that would distinguish Brian from Jesus. The three wise men attend the wrong nativity, but they also attend the right one; Jesus Christ himself appears (played by Ken Colley) at the sermon on the mount and delivers his words quite straightforwardly, it is only at the back of the crowd that confusion reigns. Later Brian's mother Mandy firmly states: 'He's not the Messiah, he's a very naughty boy.' As for the concluding mass crucifixion, research showed that this was a regular Roman punishment. When the Secretary of the British Board of Film Censors, James Ferman, first saw the film he took the view that as far as religion was concerned it was harmless, and that when a formal application for a certificate was made it would probably be awarded an 'AA'. But that was before the results of the *Gay News* appeal were known. Lord Scarman's judgment sent the Pythons back to the lawyers.

The British Board of Film Censors was in a difficult position. Although it has been in operation since 1913, it has absolutely no authority, or even existence in law. As the distinguished appeal judge Lord Denning has said: 'It is a name given to the activities of a few persons.' The real power to control the exhibition of films in the United Kingdom lies with the three-hundred-and-seventy-odd local district councils who are the licensing authorities for the cinemas in their areas. These councils control cinema buildings in terms of fire and safety, and they have absolute power to permit or forbid the showing of any film, within the constraints of the common law. Since it would be impracticable to have three-hundred-and-seventy-odd individual film censorship committees, the film exhibiting companies have established their own organization to review the contents of films, the British Board of Film Censors. The Board's recommendations are generally accepted as standard judgements for the whole country, and the practice has grown up of making cinema licenses conditional on following the recommendations of the British Board of Film Censors. However, as we shall see, district councils can always overrule the recommendations of the Board. During the 1960s the BBFC, like the BBC, moved along with the more liberal wing of public opinion as far as censorship was concerned, but, as with the BBC, this has subsequently provoked intense pressure upon it to roll back the liberal tide and return to more conservative Christian values. The *Gay News* trial showed that conservative Christian values could be enforced by law.

James Ferman was reluctant to put at risk the tenuous voluntary authority of the British Board of Film Censors by giving *The Life of Brian* a certificate, and then seeing the film condemned in a court of law for blasphemy. To make matters worse, the Festival of Light had got hold of eleven pages of the script (the Hermit scene), and was making representations to Ferman and privately propagandizing its supporters. (The Festival of Light denies that the evidence was stolen; it appears to have turned up in stray rubbish and been passed on.)

These accusations were made without the author having seen the film, but the Festival of Light was not alone in reviewing a film it had not seen. *Loki*, a 'hardline nazi magazine for all militant fascist and national socialist stormtroopers', produced this unpleasant curiosity.

FILM REVIEW CORNER

Rarely indeed, does the National Socialist come across the ultimate accolade of the film world - the wrath of the Jew! The most pernicious, evil, lavatory sex films with a multi-racial scene thrown in, fail to evoke the smallest of responses from the Jew, who can afford to relax safe in the knowledge that his own kind is profiting well from such corruption of the stupid Goyim.

However, The British made *Life of Brian* - featuring the Monty Python team has even before its release achieved this great honour; rave reviews from the Jews (literally raving!)

No less than Rabbi Abraham Hecht, President of the Rabbinical Alliance of America, is one of those Jews less than enthusiastic about *Life of Brian*. Siad Rabbi Hecht, "Monty Python's Life of Brian is blasphemous, sacriligeous and an incident to possible violence."

Foaming, he continued, "We have never come across such a foul, disgusting, blasphemous film before."

Literally gasping, he comes to the root of the matter, "Life of Brian is a vicious attack upon Judaism and the Bible and a cruel mockery of the religious feelings of Christians as well."

In the circumstances James Ferman advised the Pythons to get a barrister's opinion on the likely legal eventualities before formally submitting *The Life of Brian* for a censor's certificate.

As we saw in the case of *The Brand New Monty Python Bok*, a lawyer's opinion is still only an opinion. The first barrister to see a completed version of the film was Richard DuCann QC, who sent in a report on 24 May. Inconveniently, for the purposes of Python, he advised that for safety's sake there should be cuts. Since their intention was to reassure James Ferman that cuts were unnecessary, Mr DuCann's advice was not what they needed. There was, however, one barrister of reputation and authority who had made his position on blasphemy clear by acting for the defence in the *Gay News* trial, John Mortimer. He, if anyone, could be relied on to be favourably disposed to *Brian*, for he had taken part in a number of censorship trials and was active in support of the Defence of Literature and the Arts Society. The Pythons turned to him, and another viewing was arranged.

John Mortimer's opinion on the film did not arrive until the beginning of July, but when it did, it contained the assurances the Pythons were hoping for.

It is hard, as several judges commented, to imagine subject matter more calculated to offend Christians. Monty Phthon on the other hand, have enjoyed international success and approached the status of a world-wide comedy cult. Its individual members are household names, they are greatly admired and to many their work is irresistibly hilarious. Very significantly, "Life of Brian" is almost entirely free of references to sexuality and totally devoid of so called deviant sexuality. In these respects, "Life of Brian" seems to us to lack the essential elements of indecency and vilification.

Moreover, as the courts have emphasised, a blasphemous libel is only established if the jury finds it to be so. We feel that the likelihood of any jury convicting "Life of Brian" of such an offence to be remote. If we are right about this, two consequences flow. First, we think it puts up a considerable disincentive for even a fanatical group to institute a prosecution: secondly, it follows from our opinion that " Life of Brian" is not illegal.

6. Finally, we consider that the risk of a state prosecution is exceedingly slim. Contrary to certain public statements, the Gay News case remained a private prosecution throughout its progress in the courts and was not "taken over" by the Crown. The Director of Public Prosecutions ("the D.P.P.") did send an observer to the proceedings in the higher courts but it was clear that his department took an entirely neutral stance. We think that unless pressed by clamourous popular demand, he will in future maintain this stance, most especially where the matter complained of emanates from one of the most successful comedy teams of all time, with its own vast and enthusiastic following. These dictates of policy would only be reinforced by the dubious merits of any such prosecution. The D.P.P. would, we think, be loath to instigate such a prosecution with all its attendant raillery and publicity only for it to result in uproarious acquittal. For all these reasons, we do not think there is a substantial risk of a state prosecution. We would only wish to refer shortly to certain

7. specific scenes in the film.

Only on the next and final page did the habitual caution of the lawyer assert itself, and he warned in very general terms that the curing of the leper and the question of Mandy's virginity might give cause for complaint. Since they did not wish their case to appear weaker than it really was, the Pythons asked for an amended opinion that they could send to James Ferman. The important point was that a public prosecution was unlikely, while the Pythons' popularity and position as licensed jesters gave them better protection than a minority group like homosexuals against private prosecution by the righteous. The revised opinion was sent to the British Board of Film Censors, and arrangements were made for a formal submission of *The Life of Brian* to censorship.

The news that the film was going forward to the censors could not come a moment too soon for Geoffrey Strachan at Eyre Methuen, where plans had been laid to publish a script of the film and accompanying 'scrapbook' simultaneously with the British release of the film. The book was crashed out in five weeks in a rented apartment in Los Angeles by Eric Idle and a team of designers early in 1979, and was ready for publication in America by a New York publisher. (Again, blasphemy did not worry the American publishers in the way it did the British.)

As we saw in the case of the *Bok*, the production of elaborately illustrated books is slow and has to be planned in advance, but without a British censor's certificate there could be no release date for the film in the United Kingdom, and no British publication date for the book. Nor would there be much point in printing large numbers of the script of a film that the censors might after all ban, for whatever publicity gained would have to be set against the probability of the book being prosecuted.

Eyre Methuen's problems were compounded by the fact that the script that was ready to be published was not identical to the film to be seen on the screen. The original running time of *Brian* at the end of shooting was about two hours, too long to sustain an audience's laughter, so it had to be cut. Some of the discarded material was transferred to the scrapbook section; some of it disappeared from the film but stayed on the printed page. In the course of editing the film the Pythons themselves made changes on the grounds of taste. Much of the effing and blinding of the People's Front of Judea was cut back, because they felt they were in danger of 'losing' the audience. 'Fuck' was acceptable, but after previews, on the sound-track Reg's exasperated 'you CUNT!!!' has been changed to 'you KLUTZ!!!' John Cleese explains that this was not fear of censorship, but the foul language interfered with the comedy – and anyway 'klutz' has the same satisfying vowel sound.

The Jewish-Nazi Otto raised more sensitive issues, where the satire on contemporary Zionism, making the point that fascism and racism can exist anywhere, was bound to cause problems with the Jewish lobby in the United States, particularly since the entertainment industry contains many Jewish executives. The film had been made without any prior commitments from or to distribution companies, and without a distributor £2 million plus interest was at risk. Otto – doubtless an ardent reader of *Loki* – did not go down at all well when the film was offered to Paramount Pictures for distribution in the United States. The scene also raised problems for the action of the film, for Otto's appearance held up the story just as it was moving off into the chase. On his own initiative Eric Idle, who played the part, suggested that the sequence be cut, even though this would mean reshooting the end of the film. With the film in this form, it was accepted by Warner Communications for distribution in association with Orion Pictures, and a 'sneak preview' was arranged in Burbank, California, with minimal publicity. When the wary executives found the cinema besieged by wildly enthusiastic Python fans, they were convinced of the wisdom of their decision.

The alterations to the script were minor issues as far as Eyre Methuen were concerned, so long as the film itself was passed. Although as early as 26 April their lawyers warned about the possible consequences of printing the discarded scene between Solly and Sarah in the scrapbook section, the warning was a mild one, and Strachan decided to wait for the outcome of the main negotiations over the film itself, particularly since John Mortimer had been asked by the Pythons to give a separate opinion on the book as well. Mortimer's opinion was slow in coming, and it was June before alarm bells started to ring – in Canada.

Canada has always had a special place in *Monty Python*'s history. It was the scene of their first stage tour in 1973, but long before that the Pythons had become part of the mythology of the Canadian student revolution. The Canadian Broadcasting Corporation began transmitting *Monty Python* in the autumn of 1970 and, like the BBC on which it is modelled, CBC gave *Monty Python* as little publicity as possible. As in the United Kingdom, however, the programme quickly became a cult, particularly among students. 'Middle Canada', on the other hand took offence at the poor taste and lack of respect for revered British cultural institutions. The 'Lumberjack Song' also cast doubts on Canada's own cultural institutions, lumberjacks and Mounties, thus endearing the Pythons to students. (In Australia the singing Bruces of the Philosophical Department of the University of Woolloomooloo have done a great deal for the popularity of the Pythons there.) In January 1971 rumours began to circulate among the Canadian student population that *Monty Python* was about to be banned – and in February CBC dropped the series.

The action was too much for an American student at McGill University in Montreal, J. J. Goldberg. He wrote an article for the university newspaper calling for massive protest demonstrations outside the offices of CBC – and as luck would have it, the article was picked up by a columnist on the *Montreal Star*. Applying for a permit for the demonstration, Goldberg discovered that he had to name an organization to go with it, and instantly the Rassemblement pour Conserver Monty Python (the initials are the same as those of the Royal Canadian Mounted Police) was born.

Montreal in February, with the temperature at 20 degrees below, is no place for a demonstration, but to the RCMP's delight 200 rather than the hoped for 50 turned up. Wearing knotted handkerchiefs on their heads and shouting like St John Gumby, they paraded for two hours in the snow, doing silly walks, singing 'I'm a Lumberjack' and breaking off occasionally to shout 'Dinsdale, Dinsdale' in the hope of intimidating the people inside. Eventually a delegation was allowed into the building to talk to an executive from Programming. He listened, but gave them nothing, and in spite of simultaneous demonstrations being reported in Toronto (twenty people) and Winnipeg (six), Python for the moment stayed off the air.

In June 1979 CBC decided that it was time to ban the Pythons again. This time it was not the Pythons themselves, but a radio programme about the making of *The Life of Brian* by an eager Python fan, Mati Laansoo, who had gone out to Tunisia and recorded interviews with the group. He had also got hold of recordings of the sound-track and built them into a radio-documentary for the CBC Sunday night show, *The Entertainers*. (The Pythons had not intended that the sound-tracks be used and did not think that a programme about the film before it was released would be particularly helpful.) When CBC discovered what the show was about and heard some of the publicity for the programme, they hurriedly cancelled the broadcast. The ensuing row alerted Methuen Publications, the Canadian branch of the publishing firm in Ontario, who were also waiting to publish the film script (their copies were coming from the American printer) to coincide with the release of the film in Canada. Methuen Publications decided to seek their own legal advice.

Asked to give an opinion on the likely success or failure of a prosecution in this area, a lawyer must consider the state of public opinion as well as the technicalities of the law. John Mortimer's clearance of *Brian* for the British film censor was based on the likelihood that the reputation of *Monty Python* would make any prosecutor look absurd. In Canada – as CBC's handling of the television programmes showed – the atmosphere was different. Attitudes to censorship were more provincial; in the case of film censorship, literally so, for the ten provinces of Canada each have their own powers of censorship and exercise them in different ways. French-speaking Quebec has not exercised censorship since 1962, so that French language versions of films have played uncut in English-speaking New Brunswick, where the English language version has been cut to ribbons. Canada, like the United States, has its fundamentalist religious groups who zealously defend their view of Christianity. (One group in particular, the 'Renaissance International', led by the Reverend Ken Campbell, in 1978 helped to get a number of major Canadian literary works banned from schools in Ontario and New Brunswick.)

Methuen Publications went for their advice to Julian Porter, Canada's leading lawyer in the field of publishing. His interpretation of the book was ingenious – and alarming:

```
        In my opinion Monty Python's THE LIFE OF BRIAN
has been very cleverly drafted in light of the blasphemy
laws and the case of Regina v. Lemon.  I understand from
you that the film was commenced about three years ago
and the prosecution in Regina v. Lemon would have commenced
shortly after June of 1976.  The manuscript and the film
has been created in order to fence with the criminal laws
of blasphemy.  In short, my opinion is, although it is a
remarkably clever try it does not succeed in avoiding a
prosecution for blasphemy.  I am most concerned with the
traditional book-banning groups so long accused of
narrow-mindedness in prosecuting and persecuting books
about sex, who will jump on this book as a move to clear
their reputation.  There are a number of fundamental sects
who would, quite willingly, like to lay a charge in respect
of this book, especially in light of the decision of the
C.B.C. not to air the programme.  The test of what is a
blasphemous libel is set out in an old case, Regina v.
Hetherington which is cited in Regina v. Lemon [1979]
1 All ELR, and reads as follows:
```

After discussing various English and Canadian rulings on blasphemy, Porter issued a solemn warning:

```
            Now why do I think the manuscript is within
the confines of blasphemy?  The lawyers have very cleverly
insured that Brian of Nazareth exists at the same time as
Jesus and Jesus is introduced into the text.  It may allow
one to argue that this is just an attack on a cult and
not Christianity and that at most it was an obvious satire
on cults.  That argument has some force but I would think
a jury or a Judge would find the following matters to be
"scurrilous, offensive, contumelious abuse to sacred subjects."

            Brian (of Nazareth) born apparently in
about the year 3 A.D. (obviously the date has been changed
by three years, but the trickiness of juggling the date
will make everybody suspicious).

Page 5:      The three wise men came to visit.  The
             mother refers to the child as a brat.
             I am not aware of three wise men coming
             to visit children other than Jesus.

Page 6:      They bring the gifts of the three wise men
             and indicate that "He is the son of God, our
             Messiah."
```

He then went on to list seventeen sections of the book where the publishers were at risk.

This information was quickly communicated to Geoffrey Strachan in London, who became impatient for a sight of John Mortimer's report on the book. In Canada Methuen Publications (who had cancelled a distribution of miniature loaves and fishes at a Canadian Booksellers' Conference) were able to relax slightly when on 15 August the Ontario Board of Censors passed *The Life of Brian* with a 'restricted' rating – and made the unique proviso that all publicity for the film carried the notice: 'Warning – contents of this film may be offensive to those who have religious beliefs.' But Julian Porter stuck to his opinion. He wrote on 17 August:

```
        I am of the opinion that a judge would in fact say,
"If it is not blasphemous for the Board of Censors, then it cannot
be blasphemous for the public."  However, my opinion indicated
that there were four major areas in the second part of the book
which might be contrary to the Criminal Code.  These areas are
quite separate from the film.  So you are still taking a risk
in respect to those areas, and my opinion still stands.  However,
the overall chance of a successful prosecution is greatly
lessened by the Board of Censors' activities.
```

On the same day, protected by the first amendment to the United States constitution, *Monty Python's Life Of Brian* opened in New York, and while publication of the American version of the book went ahead happily, the imminent release of the film in Canada increased the pressure on Methuen Publications.

In London the problem was even worse, for there the books had not been printed yet, and if *Brian* did get past the censors there would be little time to produce it to coincide with the film's release. It was a slight relief to hear from Sydney that while Australia and each of its states had blasphemy laws, none had been used for a hundred years, and Associated Book Publishers (Australia) did not expect them to be used now. However, on 2 August Strachan had at last received a copy of John Mortimer's opinion on the book. The report homed in on the same dangerous areas in the scrapbook section identified by Julian Porter.

```
a)  The dialogue between Boley and Sarah in which Sarah
    alleges she is pregnant by the Holy Ghost : who is
    described as a 'Horny little poltergeist' I have
    discussed this with those instructing me and I think
    it can be argued that this passage is merely the comic
    excuse of a silly girl who has got herself pregnant.
    It is also clear the actual seducer was not infact the
    Holy Ghost but an ordinary mortal with a penchant
    for underage girls.  I feel a little nervous about
    this page as it could well be alleged, as I think
    wrongly, that it is an attack on the somewhat nebulous
    personage who is held to be a member of the Christian
    Trinity.

              - 2 -

    If the publishers wish to take every precaution they
    would remove this page; but if they do not I think
    it could be defended successfully against a charge
    of blasphemy.

b)  The ex-leper scene.  I have discussed this with those
    instructing me.  On the page 13 I think we should cut
    the word "( Gestures in the manner of a conjuror)
    You're cured mate sod you"and in paragraph 14 cut the
    ex-leper's second speech after about to become a goat
    herd, removing "Just because some long-haired conjuror
    starts mucking about (makes gesture again) Just like
    that "You're cured bloody do gooder"

              The description of Christ as a Conjuror are too
    close to the blasphemy alleged in R v Gott (1922 16
    C.A.R. 86) to be safe in my opinion.

c)  I have dealt with the suggestion that Brian's mother
    was a virgin and its closeness to the virgin birth of
    Christ and said that it should be removed from the film.
    It should also come out of the book.  It is on a page
    which is numbered 47 and we should cut from " She
    propels him out of sight " to "BRIAN opens the door
    leading downstairs.
```

SOLLY What do you mean, the Holy Ghost?

SARAH I said, the Holy Ghost done it.

SOLLY He got you up the gut, the Holy Ghost did?

SARAH Yeah.

SOLLY You expect me to believe that the Holy Ghost took a night off from heaven, came down to number 42, Sheep Way, and shacked up with you.

SARAH Yeah.

SOLLY Let me get this right—the Spiritual ruler of the entire Universe feeling a touch randy and in need of a bit of the other, manifests himself, comes down and nips in to bed with you.

SARAH Yeah.

SOLLY Nice one. I don't get a bit of nooky out of you for two years and next thing you're having knee tremblers with a bloody archangel.

SARAH He's not a bloody archangel he's the Holy Ghost.

SOLLY Oh yeah—if the Holy Ghost climbs into bed with you—it's down with the sheets and on with the job. If it's me, it's no, not till after we're married, we must save it up it's precious.

SARAH It's true.

SOLLY It's so fucking precious you give it to every horny little poltergeist that comes banging on the bedroom door.

SARAH Only one.

SOLLY Oh only one. Sorry, not the Trinity. Three persons in one bed; no, just one sexy little seraph at a time. Sorry Solly I'm saving my cherry for a cherub.

SARAH I couldn't turn him down he's the Holy Ghost.

SOLLY What did he look like, did he have his head tucked under his arm?

SARAH He's not that sort of a ghost.

SOLLY How do I know what sort of a ghost he is. I've not been to bed with the buggers. Madame Poilu's all I get for two years, not you no, you've got your feet in the air, being humped by Heavenly visitors.

SARAH It was spiritual.

SOLLY If it was so spiritual how come he's left his little gift in you.

SARAH It's a blessing.

SOLLY I notice he doesn't stay around for the blessing. Oh no, far too busy dipping his holy wick in the lamps of foolish virgins. I mean I feel frankly, that if the Holy Ghost is going around shagging all and sundry the least he can do is stick around and see his offspring through the crèche stage.

SARAH He said I was to tell you and you'd understand and marry me.

SOLLY I see. I see. So my idea of the perfect wife is supposed to be someone who puts out for any dissipated sprite who fancies getting his end away with the scarlet women of the spiritual world.

SARAH He was the Holy Ghost.

SOLLY I don't care if he's the Holy Choir Invisible. I don't want any lecherous apparitions unsheathing their pork swords in my sheets.

SARAH He was ever so nice. He said I could call him Brian.

SOLLY Brian.

SARAH Yes.

SOLLY Brian, the Holy Ghost.

SARAH Yes.

SOLLY And do you recollect throughout two thousand years of scripture the Holy Ghost ever being referred to previously as Brian.

SARAH Erm no.

SOLLY So it never crossed your mind that this smutty seraphim, this rampant genie with his pants round his ankles, might perhaps not be an angel of the most high in rut but some quite ordinary mortal with a gift of the gab and a penchant for banging underage briffit.

SARAH I've never done it before.

SOLLY I'm afraid my dear you've fallen for a very old line.

PAUSE

SARAH Do you want me to show you what he did?

SOLLY What?

SARAH Do you want me to show you what he taught me?

SOLLY What all the way? Bareback?

SARAH I can't get more pregnant can I?

SOLLY No.

SARAH Somebody's got to be second.

SOLLY Yeah.

SARAH It's ever so nice.

SOLLY All right.

SARAH Between you and me, I never fancied him that much.

SOLLY No?

SARAH No, it wasn't very big.

SOLLY That's not supposed to count.

SARAH I know. But it helps.

Geoffrey Strachan had seriously to consider Eyre Methuen's position. At this stage the final deal for publishing the book had not been made. (Strachan was negotiating with Denis O'Brien and the film's production film company, HandMade Films.) It was clear that the content of the book of the film was technically running far greater risks than the film itself, but Eyre Methuen's position – should they try to ask for changes – was seriously weakened by the fact that neither the film nor the book had been cut in the United States. Informal talks with the Pythons were difficult to arrange, for they had dispersed to the four corners of the world, and Eric Idle in particular was sticking to his usual policy of keeping out of the way once the creative editorial work was done. Strachan faced up to the dilemma in a letter of 8 August to Eyre Methuen's lawyer, Michael Rubinstein:

We must consider carefully our position vis a vis the authors. Our ability to take a convincing firm stand over Mortimer's suggested cuts is, I believe, in some ways weakened by the fact that the book and the film as they stand (without "bowdlerization") are being published and shown in America.

We can certainly do our best to urge them to follow John Mortimer's advice and I believe that the most persuasive argument is that the bringing of a prosecution could damage sales of the book even if it were ultimately unsuccessful.

It is conceivable, however, that if the Pythons refuse to alter a line I and my colleagues might feel inclined to run the risk of publishing the book in the U.K. as it stands. It would be useful to know the "worst" that might happen to us (length of likely prison sentence for myself; size of find for A.B.P. as principal conspirator; assessment of likely costs of a case; any other costs?; seizure and destruction of stock?) were a prosecution to be brought and prove to be successful. If one page were deemed to be blasphemous could the book be reissued without it? Is there any way in which the Pythons could give evidence in court?

Strachan received a rapid reply:

If you were to take a risk of publishing here on the Pythons refusal to accept the alteration of a line let along the deletion of a page, I do not believe that there is any serious risk at all of a prison sentence: at worst, no-one should receive a prison sentence not immediately suspended. An aggregate of fines in case of conviction should not exceed £1,000 (unless at the time inflation or any other exacerbating cause boosted that figure) but costs of defending might be anything between £15,000 and £30,000 or more (especially if an acquittal were to result only after an appeal). If a prosecution for blasphemy were to relate to only one page then the book could be re-issued without that. The Pythons might give evidence in court if prosecuted with you but in the Gay News case the intention of a blasphemous author was held irrelevant and therefore not to be given by way of evidence.

One possibility was that HandMade Films might be persuaded to give some sort of guarantee that would indemnify Eyre Methuen for the losses of a court case, but Rubinstein pointed out that blasphemy was a criminal offence, and it is not possible to indemnify a person against the penalties of a crime he has committed. Strachan once more considered his options:

PYTHON POSITION 13.8.79

1. Wait for film to get certificate in U.K.
   If awarded without cuts ignore advice on screenplay.
   (If Pythons decide to cut virgin scene ask to cut from book)
   Don't sign contract or print till certificate awarded.

2. With regard to other cuts 'recommended' by Mortimer.
   Publish & be damned.

3. Accept Rubinstein advice on Warranty clause &
   sign contract.

4. Press for publication as early before
   the film release as no pythons will agree to.

486·7625

74

At this stage Strachan had reluctantly come round to the view that in the interests of getting the book out on time, he was going to have to ask the Pythons to make cuts, a proposal he put more formally to the personal manager of Python Productions, Anne Henshaw, the following day:

I am afraid we are firmly of the opinion (and are advised in this sense) that it would be rash in the extreme for us merely to shrug off, or to recommend to the Pythons that we shrug off, the cautions and advice of a Q.C. specializing in this field without giving further consideration to the technical implications of the law as it stands (however abhorrent). The implication of Mortimer's opinion appears to be that there is a clear risk, in the current climate of opinion, that a fanatical puritan could bring a prosecution (most likely against ourselves as publishers), the effects of which might be to involve Eyre Methuen in hugely costly litigation, which could add a considerable financial burden to our substantial initial investment in the book and, worst of all, might prevent us from publishing and selling the book freely at the moment of greatest demand, to the considerable financial detriment of the authors as well as ourselves.

I regret enormously that we had to wait four months following May 1st to reach this stage. But this has happened. Now, for the sake of the book, which could go drastically off schedule with the printers if we don't reach a resolution soon, there is little doubt that a quick decision to follow Mortimer's advice with regard to 'Solly and Sarah', the ex-Leper scene and the 'Virgin' scene could probably resolve the matter faster than anything else (though substitute copy for the 'Solly and Sarah' page would have to be found. And while I hate suggesting cuts to passages I happen to like I think it could fairly be said that the pleasure many thousands of readers will take in the book as a whole, would vary hardly at all as a result.

As an alternative, Strachan suggested a grand conference involving Eyre Methuen and Michael Rubinstein, with John Mortimer and as many of the Pythons as possible. He hoped to be able to reconcile the conflicting opinions of the lawyers and to thrash out what might or might not be done in the event of a prosecution. The Pythons, now alerted to the extreme anxiety displayed by their publisher, could not see what good a conference would do. Among themselves they decided not to give in to censorship, delegating Michael Palin to telephone Strachan with the news. There was to be no meeting and the book, if it was to be published in the United Kingdom, was to be published as it stood.

At this point, in the last week of August, the British Board of Film Censors finally made up their minds about *Brian*. The film was first viewed by four of the six examiners at the end of July but there was a further delay until the Board's President, Lord Harlech, also viewed it. The decision was to ask for absolutely no cuts at all, and to rate the film 'AA'.

The news forced a decision on Eyre Methuen. It was now likely that the film would be released before Christmas (it was thought prudent, well *before* Christmas) and the book would have to be ready in time. In Canada the film was running, but the books were still in the warehouse. In London the firm must decide whether to print, and quickly. On 6 September Geoffrey Strachan put the case for a contract and publication to the senior directors of Eyre Methuen's parent company, Associated Book Publishers.

I have been to some pains in recommending to the Python that we take
seriously from a practical point of view the caution advocated on these technical
matters by Rubinstein and Mortimer (in the case of one passage Denis O'Brien of
Hand Made Films, with whom our contract will be made, attempted this himself, but withdrew,
defeated from the field).

However the Pythons have, as I understand it, reached the conclusion after
long and careful discussion amongst themselves, as well as with me, that the suggested
cuts are irrelevant to the central issues: 1.) have they made a good funny film and
a good funny book (irreverent but not in any way cruel or beastly to living
individuals)? 2.) will the film and the book be successful as they stand? They are
convinced that the answer to both is 'yes'. I agree with them.

I am convinced that we now have to choose between publishing the book as
it stands to coincide with the film and backing out - as a result of which we could
only forfeit all further books by the Pythons, individually and collectively (which
during the past few years have been quite crucial to the success of the Eyre Methuen
list). We should, I think, also incur great odium amongst the writing community
generally, being seen as publishers of many avant-garde and radical writers who were too timid
to say 'boo' to the Festival of Light.

I am not a Christian(nor am I a Buddhist, a Jew or a Muslim) but I am
convinced that there is nothing in either the film or the book which is truly a
blasphemy against the human spirit or the spirit of the divine in man. Both are

Associated Book Publishers backed Strachan's judgment and the contract with HandMade Films was made.

Everyone, however, had reckoned without the printers. The Severn Valley Press, who had had the book ready to print since the end of July, now took their own legal advice. Instead of going to the lawyer most likely to recommend publication, they went to the lawyer most likely to advise against, John Smyth, the successful prosecutor in the *Gay News* case and an advisor to the Festival of Light. He found the book scurrilous, indecent and offensive, and warned seriously against printing it. It was now too late to find different printers altogether, but the scrapbook half of the book was trucked away from the Severn Valley Press in Pontygwindy, Caerphilly, to Sir Joseph Causton & Sons in Eastleigh, Hampshire. And that is why the first impression of *Monty Python's The Life of Brian (of Nazareth)* has one printer and *Montypythonscrapbook* has another.

Most of the censorial decisions recorded in this chapter were taken in private; they were business decisions based on estimates of likely public opinion. And though sections of the community were hard at work to form opinion against *Brian*, the public had yet to have a chance to make up its own mind.

There is a sequel to the most personal decision of all, Lord Delfont's refusal to finance the film. When the film was ready for release, it was offered for distribution to CIC, which has its own theatre in the West End of London, but uses primarily EMI-owned cinemas when a film goes on general release. Late in 1979 at the last shareholders' meeting before the financially ailing EMI merged with Thorn Electrical Industries Ltd, Lord Delfont still insisted that the film was blasphemous. But EMI cinemas up and down the country showed the film all the same.

IS THIS
THE MOST
BLASPHEMOUS
FILM EVER?

Evening News

VI

'This squalid little film'

Malcolm Muggeridge

Monty Python's Life of Brian was given its world première on 17 August 1979 at Cinema One on New York's Third Avenue. Once Warner Communications, together with Orion Pictures, had agreed to distribute the film there were no fears about direct censorship in the United States, for the Pythons' freedom of expression was enshrined in the first amendment to the Constitution:

> Congress shall make no law respecting an establishment of religion, or prohibiting the free exercise thereof; or abridging the freedom of speech, or of the press; or the right of the people peaceably to assemble, and to petition the Government for the redress of grievances.

Freedom of religion and freedom of speech go together. Since the United States was founded by people who wanted to find freedom of religious expression, it is a country where there are strong feelings about the freedom of the individual to express his views. But as the Pythons soon discovered, no less strong are the feelings about religion.

With no established church, America has many competing sects. In recent years fundamentalist evangelical groups relying on the charisma of television and radio preachers have gained ground against older and more traditional churches. While fiercely defending their own rights to religious expression, some fundamentalist groups are less liberal towards the rights of expression of others, for conservative Christianity tends to go with political conservatism. A case in point is Jerry Falwell's independent Baptist church in Lynchberg, Virginia: his 'Old Time Gospel Hour' is carried by 700 radio and television stations to an estimated audience of twenty-one million; in 1979 Falwell created Moral Majority, an overtly political organization that backed President Reagan's campaign for election. Moral Majority, like the California-based Christian Voice, like the Round Table and the National Christian Action Coalition, opposes liberal abortion laws and the relaxation of penalties for homosexuality; they seek to control sex education in schools (some groups oppose the teaching of Darwinian theories of evolution, preferring the Bible's account of creation) and resist equal rights

legislation for women. As we shall see, the Pythons' constitutional rights may be protected at national level, but could be curtailed locally by a combination of political and religious pressure. (Religious fanaticism, however, has proved its own enemy, for in 1979 it was less than twelve months since a fundamentalist sect had committed mass suicide at Jonestown, Guyana.)

Strictly speaking, there is no film censorship in the United States. The Motion Picture Association of America runs a Classification and Ratings Administration which rates the films voluntarily submitted to it on a fourfold scale from 'G' to 'X', but this rating is purely advisory and only intended to inform parents as to what to expect. The much stricter (though technically still voluntary) censorship exercised by the Hays Office was given up in 1968, after a franker and more realistic kind of film-making established itself in the 1960s. *The Life of Brian* was rated 'R' for restricted, meaning that children under the age of 17 should be accompanied by an adult. The judgment of the New York critics on *Brian* was generally favourable, but the Pythons were attacked from positions right across the religious spectrum.

The first protest came almost immediately, on 19 August, from the President of the Rabbinical Alliance of America, Rabbi Benjamin Hecht. The Rabbinical Alliance is extremely conservative – 'ultra-orthodox' – as are the two other Jewish organizations Hecht was also speaking for, the Union of Orthodox Rabbis of the United States and Canada, and the Rabbinical Council of Syrian and Near Eastern Sephardic Communities of America. Claiming to represent 1,000 rabbis and half a million Jews, Hecht denounced *Brian* as sacrilege and blasphemy. 'This film is so grievously insulting that we are genuinely concerned that its continued showing could result in violence.' The dispassionate observer might be led to think that the threat of violence came from those protesting against the film rather than the film itself, but Hecht argued that people 'might be moved to violence because it is a bad movie . . . I have an idea that it was produced in Hell.'

Rabbi Hecht's denunciation was quickly joined by the Protestant voice of Robert E. A. Lee, who produced a syndicated radio commentary for the Lutheran Council. A thousand radio stations across America carried Lee's comment that Brian was 'crude and rude mockery, colossal bad taste, profane parody' and 'a disgraceful and distasteful assault on religious sensitivity'. Not to be outdone, the Roman Catholic Office for Film and Broadcasting rated *Brian* 'C' for condemned, making it a sin to see the film. The Catholic Film Office (originally the Catholic National Legion of Decency) felt that the once powerful influence of its twice-monthly film *Review* was slipping. The Office no longer supported the Motion Picture Association's rating system; over *Brian* its director, Father Sullivan, protested: 'The code as a yardstick has long been abandoned, leaving nothing more than a convenient rating system. We still would have expected that at least the spirit of the old code would have been operative. We would have expected an "X" rating.' Father Sullivan was backed up by the Roman Catholic Archdiocese of New York, which declared that *Brian* 'holds the person of Christ up to comic ridicule and is, for Christians, an act of blasphemy.' For the Archdiocese, Father Jadoff said: 'This is the most blasphemous film I have ever seen and it pretends to be nothing else.' The Pythons could only conclude that they had made an unwitting contribution to religious reconciliation and church unity. *The Life of Brian* meanwhile broke box office records at Cinema One.

It must be pointed out that the religious groups who condemned the film were themselves criticized by others. The Executive Vice-President of the Conservative Rabbinical Assembly, Rabbi Wolfe Kelman, warned: 'Any attempt by any central group to impose a boycott is very dangerous for the freedom of ideas.' The National Council of Churches, representing thirty-one Protestant groups, took a liberal view of the whole affair. At the NCC Dr William Fore, Chairman of the National Coalition Against Censorship, said: 'There has been no protest here, and we're not contemplating any.' Other people, however, were.

Those most offended by *Brian* formed a Citizens Against Blasphemy Committee and hired lawyers to try to bring a prosecution against the film. The lawyers were unsuccessful, but on 16 September a remarkable variety of religious groups gathered to protest outside the Warner Communications building at the Rockerfeller Center, and then march on Cinema One.

The Rabbinical Alliance, the Brooklyn diocesan Holy Name Society and the Nassau County Chapter of the Catholic League for Religious and Civil Rights were all represented. The Orthodox Church was represented by Bishop Gregory of the Russian Orthodox Church Outside Russia, and the evangelical Protestants by the Reverend Roger Fulton of the Neighbourhood Church in Greenwich Village. (Fulton's anti-homosexual stance has caused him considerable conflict with his neighbourhood.) Fulton's four-page speech gives an idea of the rhetoric used against *Brian*. It also shows how deeply worrying the English music-hall tradition of men dressing up in women's clothing is to some Americans. A political element

Address of Rev. Roger Fulton
(Pastor, Neighborhood Church, NYC)
At the Citizens Against Blasphemy Rally
In front of Warner Communications Bldg.
Sunday, September 16, 1979

EXACTLY WHY WE OBJECT TO THE "BRIAN" FILM

The Prophet Isaiah cried out: "Woe to those determined to drag their sins around with them like a cart on a rope. Some of them even mock the Holy One of Israel and dare the Lord to punish them. 'Hurry and punish us, O Lord,' they say; 'we want to see what You can do!' Woe to those who call what is evil good and what is good evil....Woe to those who are wise and shrewd in their own eyes ....Woe to those who undermine the rightness of those who are in the right."

A few evenings ago I endured, for research and evaluation purposes, almost two full showings of what I feel can be aptly referred to as Monty Snake's "Life of Brian." My general reaction and sentiments are ably expressed in a tiny letter that appeared in last Thursday's New York Post. Mr. Joseph P. LaRuffa of Brooklyn wrote:

"The writers, makers and distributing agents of the vulgar, anti-Christian and anti-Semitic film, 'The Life of Brian,' need new brains!"

I might add: "...and a new heart, a new soul and a new spirit!"

When I arrived home from Cinema I the other night, my remark to my wife and neighbors about the film was, "The half has never yet been told." I had been hearing and reading small dribs and drabs of what is in this motion picture, but when I saw it, I said to myself, "Why don't we really tell what is in it, so that the God-fearing majority in this area and across the land will become totally aroused?"

From the notes I wrote in large letters on a scratch pad in the dark movie house, I have prepared four lists representing four categories of outrageously objectionable material in "The Life of Brian." I'm certain there is widespread agreement among many of us here today concerning the great majority of these points. Let me share them with you.

The first category is Immoral Aspects of the Film.

The mother of Messiah (Brian) is a man in woman's clothing, in direct violation of the Holy Scriptures.

The film blatantly tosses about almost every vile four-letter word known in gutter English.

The mother of Messiah reports that she was raped and eventually found it pleasant.

Several times male desires to change into a female are expressed.

Patriots are pictured crawling through a hole in a private bodily area shown in a large mosaic, supposedly to reach the quarters of Pontius Pilate's wife and murder her.

entered the protestors' speeches: the President of Orion Pictures, Arthur Krim, whose company was distributing the film with Warner Communications, is a senior member of the Democratic Party. Appeals were made to President Carter to sack this 'promoter of sacrilege', though by association the target for the attack was the Democratic Party itself.

The protests against Krim or *Brian* at Cinema One were ineffectual, but in Brooklyn the manager of the Fortway Theater gave in to locally organized protest and decided that it would not be prudent to show the film. 'We don't want the community to be offended,' he explained, taking a line that was soon to be heard from managers right across the country.

Two days after the rally, as the Citizens Against Blasphemy Committee began a campaign to restore to the statute book of the State of New York a blasphemy law dropped in 1967, the connection between Christian and conservative objections to *Brian* was reinforced by a widely syndicated article for the *New York Post* from the celebrated right-wing columnist William F. Buckley. The choice of *Monty Python* as a subject was more important than what Buckley actually said; his understanding of the film did not appear to be total; indeed he may not have even seen the film, for he seemed to think that a character called Monty Python was being crucified in the final scene. (This, however, was better than those who claimed that Christ is also in the mass execution.) Buckley's main target is Richard Shickel of *Time* magazine, whose review of the film suggested that the protests 'will attract those who need it most: adults who have not had their basic premises offended, and thereafter have not examined them, in too long.'

The suggestion that people should be challenged to reconsider their assumptions was too much for the conservative Mr Buckley:

We are told that all our basic premises need occasionally to be 'offended'. Well, one of our basic premises is that people ought not to be persecuted on account of their race or religion. Is Mr Shickel saying that we should have an occasional holocaust? Or is he saying that if we go for a stretch of time without a holocaust, at least we ought to engage the Monty Python players to do a comedy based on Auschwitz? With the characters marching into the gas chamber dancing, say, the mamba? Led by Anne Frank?

William Buckley's question-marks avoid a direct statement and his hyperbole distorts Shickel's meaning, but it was an effective smear. Further to the right, the John Birch Society's weekly magazine condemned *Brian*, whereas the *Nation*, the most left-leaning of the major journals, thought *Brian* potentially more offensive to homosexuals than to anyone else. In California the *Long Beach Independent* produced perfect balance by condemning *Brian* on the religious page, and then publishing a favourable film review a week later.

William Buckley's article was quickly picked up by the Interfaith Committee Against Blasphemy, based in Glendale, California. Describing itself as 'a group of southern California Catholic and Protestant clergy', the Committee made a point of protesting against films treating critically of religion. It had campaigned against Thorsen's proposed *The Many Faces of Jesus* and produced a television programme presented by the singer Pat Boone, *Those Sacrilegious Movies*. Having already warned against *Brian* in its February 1979 newsletter, it now circulated a four-page attack on *Brian* which shows how a pressure group organizes a campaign – and finances it. Such campaigns work

> Your tax-deductible gift of $1,000, $500, $100 or even smaller amounts . . . whatever you feel God wants you to invest, will be used to research, to document, to keep our people informed and to launch all-out Christian opposition against commercialized blasphemy. This is not a charity, but rather an honest effort by people of many faiths, joining together in a common goal. We earnestly need your help.
>
> God bless you!

most successfully when they are able to convince people that the film is shocking before they have had a chance to see it, and it is true of most of the objectors to *Brian* that they are going on distorted hearsay. (One rumour had it that a child was mutilated during the film.) The Interfaith Committee Against Blasphemy, however, was not the only organization spreading the word against *Brian*: the *Cultural Information Service*, a magazine funded by the Episcopal Church, Presbyterian Church, United Church of Christ and the United Presbyterian Church, told its readers: 'this movie is sacrilegious'. The Evangelical Sisterhood of Mary circulated anti-*Brian* material from Phoenix, Arizona; the Committee Against Indiscriminate Display of Pornography organized protests in Massachusetts; in several places Morality in Media, in which the anti-abortion, anti-homosexual campaigner Barbara Anderson has been prominent, were active against the film.

The true test of *The Life of Brian* began when, having established itself in the big centres like New York and Los Angeles, on 19 September the film began to be shown across the country by the Boston-based General Cinema Corporation, the largest single chain with 850 theatres coast to coast. Predictably, trouble began when *Brian* arrived in the south-eastern states of the so-called Bible Belt, where fundamentalist religion and reactionary politics flourish. After Brooklyn, the first cancellation was in Charlotte, North

YOUR RIGHTS HAVE BEEN VIOLATED!

Our rights are being violated! Local ministers are violating our First Amendment rights. They have successfully caused the ban of the new Monty Python movie, "Life of Brian." These ministers and their supporters, according to the Charlotte Observer, have not even seen the movie. They have assumed that because the movie is uncongenial to their personal beliefs and opinions it is uncongenial to everyone's beliefs and opinions. This is an obvious misconception. Ours is a country of multivaried viewpoints and free choice. Those who chose not to see the movie have a perfect right to make such a choice, but they do not have the right to deny the opposite choice to those who might wish to see it. Church authorities do not have the power under law to decide for everyone what they'll be allowed to see, hear, and read. When they attempt to do so, they are violating the First Amendment of the Constitution.

The violation of our First Amendment rights is far more dangerous to our community than the showing of what a few people consider an offensive movie.

Concerned peoples wishing to protest this ban will be at Eastland Mall Cinema at 11:00 p.m. tonight and every night until the ban is lifted. Also, concerned people will boycott all General Cinema Theatres until the ban is lifted. The Cinemas in Charlotte are at Eastland, SouthPark, and Charlottetown. If you wish to protest directly to General Cinema Theatres Corp., call Chestnut Hill, Mass. at 617-232-8200.

CONCERNED CITIZENS

Carolina. A protest led by a local Baptist minister, who had not seen the film, was enough to secure a hurried cancellation of the scheduled showing of *Brian*. The citizens of Charlotte were given a chance to see *Killer Fish* instead.

Across the border in Columbia, South Carolina, *Brian* opened on 19 October – and closed again the next day. South Carolina is the fief of the seventy-eight-year-old Republican Senator Strom Thurmond, in the 1960s an opponent of civil rights for blacks, a critic of the abortion laws and an unequivocal supporter of capital punishment. Since President Reagan's election Senator Thurmond has become Chairman of the Senate Judiciary Committee. When *Brian* arrived in Columbia a local Presbyterian minister telephoned Thurmond's wife Nancy to complain. Thurmond immediately got in touch with General Cinema's head office and had a quiet word with their attorney, Samuel Frankenheim. Said Frankenheim: 'Thurmond called me and apprised me of a potentially explosive situation in Columbia. He communicated an overwhelming community sentiment against the film.' The cancellation, however, provoked counter-protests. Pickets appeared at the cinema with signs reading: 'Let Us Decide', 'Resurrect Brian, Crucify Censors'. State Representative Bill Campbell joined in: 'Senator Thurmond told the General Cinema people that his folks take their religion seriously. I called them and told them we take our freedoms very seriously too.'

The General Cinema people found the going tough. In Louisiana *Brian* was already running in Metaire when, also on 19 October, it was taken off, and General Cinema cancelled showings scheduled in Alexandria, Shreveport, Lafayette and Lake Charles. The Louisiana troubles had begun in Baton Rouge, where the District Attorney, Ossie Brown (who was about to stand for re-election), used the threat of a prosecution for obscenity to discourage a showing there. He lifted the threat of prosecution after a private viewing of the film, but the film stayed off. District Attorney Brown's influence spread to Slidell, Louisiana, where the film *had* opened on 19th, but with the help of their mayor and assistant district attorney, the Slidell Ministerial Alliance got the film taken off again. The district attorney at Houma viewed the film but made no comment, in Louisiana and only there and at Hammond were the showings trouble-free. Ossie Brown's activities were so effective in keeping *Brian* out of most of Louisiana that Warner Communications threatened to take out an injunction against him.

Similar pressures came into play in Mississippi, where *Brian* closed in Jackson after a week, when the district attorney warned the cinema manager that there might be violence if the cinema were picketed. Mississippi is the base of fundamentalist Donald Wildman's National Federation for Decency; his protest was to send back his American Express card cut in half because he believed erroneously that American Express had helped to finance *Brian*. In Arkansas local pressure prevented showings at Russellville, Hot Springs, North Little Rock and Conway, and the local press commented that the exhibitors did not even try to get *Brian* shown in Fort Smith. Discouraged by the trouble caused by pickets and protests, cinema managers became more and more reluctant to book *Brian* in the first place.

The protests, however, were not confined to the Bible Belt and demonstrations shortened runs in Massachusetts, Maine and Michigan. In California campaigners began to protest sometimes weeks after the film had begun its run without controversy. Prominent among the protesters was Mrs Marian Banducci, an anti-abortionist and unsuccessful Congressional candidate. Her United Christians started to picket the Clay Theater in San Francisco five weeks after *Brian* opened; they then moved on to Fremont. Outreach for Christ picketed in Bakersfield, the Interfaith Committee Against Blasphemy inspired pickets in Anderson; the National Federation for Decency contributed pickets at Davis.

Decisions on the fate of *Brian* were taken at local level, in accordance with managers' estimates of the amount of provocation the film would cause. Some may have felt like the owner of the Rowan cinemas in Salisbury, North Carolina, who took the film off 'because it was personally offensive to me', but others were prepared to resist hostile public opinion. In New York State the Roman Catholic Bishop of Ogdensburg, Stanislaus Brzana, a keen supporter of Morality in Media, encouraged worshippers at St Mary's Cathedral and Notre Dame Church to sign a petition against *Brian.* A prayer meeting was held outside the Ogdensburg Twin Cinemas when the film opened on 2 November and the following day Bishop Brzana personally led a seventy-person picket. The cinema management kept the film on and hung out a sign: 'Honk if you love Brian'.

Some managers showed ingenious deference to local opinion. At Great Falls, Montana, Carisch Theaters organized a poll at its four cinemas and a three-to-one vote in favour secured *Brian* a showing. In Hobbs, New Mexico the Hobbs Commonwealth Cinema organized a preview for civil and religious leaders after a petition against the film was got up in the town. After the show a ballot was held, though sadly the results were not divulged because, the management said, 'the decision to show the movie was taken at a higher level'. At Laconia, New Hampshire the Colonial Theater's owner, Richard Beaupré, first cancelled *Brian* and then, when he saw the controversy – and interest – he had caused, rebooked.

The threat of legal action, as at Fort Walton, Florida, was sometimes enough to have the film withdrawn, but no serious attempt to bring *Brian* to book succeeded. In Oklahoma the state's blasphemy law had been applied as recently as 1941, but the demonstrators who paraded carrying wooden crosses outside the Woodland Hills Cinema in Tulsa were disappointed when the District Attorney decided that no action could be taken. At Valdosta, Georgia, Judge Ray Lilley granted an injunction against *Brian* on 19 October but reversed it the next day after he had seen the film. The injunction was sought by ten church groups on the grounds that the film was obscene, primarily because of the 'lewd exhibition of genitals'. This was, however, only a legal ploy, as the Reverend Gary Folds, the Baptist minister leading the protest, explained: 'We're not trying to make it a religious issue, although it certainly is.'

Before opening in Provo, Utah, *Brian* was previewed and passed by one of the strictest local censorship panels in the country. By chance the chairman of the panel, Stephen West, had missed the preview, and after a subsequent viewing demanded that the Provo District Attorney should ban the film and charge the cinema manager with blasphemy. The DA viewed the film, 'laughed throughout' and did nothing. In Waco, Texas, where the Ivy Theater received a bomb threat because of *Brian*, the legal adviser to the Waco police recommended that no action should be taken against the film. The handful of anti-*Brian* pickets outside the cinema were countered by an equal handful of *Brian* supporters. In Massachusetts Boston Municipal Court Judge John A. Pinto ruled at the beginning of December that *Brian* might be boring, but it was not blasphemous and did not violate the state's three-hundred-year-old blasphemy law. Across the frontier at Sault Sainte Marie in Canada, the Reverend Michael Eldred of St Joseph Island started a private prosecution against the local cinema, but the Ontario Attorney General stopped the case before hearings began: on the grounds that 'it was not in the interests of the administration of justice' to proceed.

It is impossible to say how many cinema managers decided not to book *Brian* for fear of protests, though the actual cancellations are far outnumbered by the theatres where *Brian* was shown without trouble. It is clear that exhibitors were – and still are – seriously discouraged in the American Bible Belt and in the more conservative areas of Canada but in several cities the film was taken up by another chain after the original renters gave in to local pressure. This happened in Charlotte and Hickory, North Carolina, and in Columbia and other cities in South Carolina, in spite of Senator Thurmond's influence. The protesters have also to consider the benefits of publicity that they brought to *Brian*. Whether the Pythons intended it or not, the controversy had a healthy effect on the box office. To date the total American box office receipts are estimated to be over $27 million (of course, as with all film finance, only a fraction of this sum will ever reach the Pythons).

The film's successful progress was particularly galling to John Heyman, the producer of the lugubriously respectful *Jesus*, also distributed by Warner Communications and put on general release not long after *Brian*. In several cities *Jesus* found itself playing in the same cinema complex as *The Life of Brian*. Heyman considered this most unfair treatment by Warner Communications and spoke of suing his distributor: 'I question the business methods of a company that will self-evidently invite horrendous comparisons.'

In commercial terms, however, the true mark of *Brian*'s success was imitation. The *San Francisco Examiner* reported on 20 October that David Begelman and Freddie Fields were 'hurriedly preparing for the production of *Wholly Moses. Moses* will be another religious spoof . . .'.

The controversy caused by *Brian* in America was reported in the United Kingdom, where the supporters and opponents of the film were preparing to do battle on the different ground created by the terms of British film censorship. The 'AA' certificate granted without cuts in August gave the first round to the Pythons, and their opponents may have concluded that the publicity created in America was counterproductive. The chief opposition came from the Nationwide Festival of Light – Mrs Whitehouse wrote to the *Evening Standard* in October to point out that, contrary to reports, neither she nor the National Viewers' and Listeners' Association had made any comment on *The Life of Brian*. As we saw in the last chapter, at the beginning of 1979 the Festival of Light was lobbying the British Board of Film Censors to refuse a certificate, but with an opening scheduled in London for 8 November, the tone of the Festival of Light's propaganda changed.

At the end of October the Festival of Light issued a warning against 'over-reaction' to the film: 'It does not constitute blasphemy in the full and strict sense. It is now clear that *Brian* is not, and could not reasonably be taken to be a cartoon caricature of our Lord. Separate birth scenes make this clear.' Since the Festival of Light had still not seen the film (their director was excluded from a preview), 'this must remain a *provisional* judgement', but it concluded that it was 'extremely unlikely that the film would sustain a successful prosecution'. The Festival of Light therefore recommended a more discreet – almost sinister – approach to hampering the film:

> The makers may even be hoping that we condemn it outright, just to give it extra free publicity! We suggest therefore that any action taken locally should be low-key – i.e. avoiding media coverage, restrained in tone, and written as tentative suggestion using some of the above facts and comments.

(c)   The viewing committee may come to one of three possible decisions:

(i)   to leave the film with an 'AA' certificate and risk the consequences;

(ii)   to change the certificate to 'X' – meaning only those over 18 may see the film; or

(iii)   to ban the film entirely from the local cinemas.

(d)   It should be stressed that a total ban on a violent or obscene film (which the B.B.F.C. has certificated) is not an unusual occurrence in a number of local authority areas, from industrial Yorkshire to Cornwall.   Furthermore, the Home Office model licensing conditions, which most local authorities use when licensing cinemas annually, lay an obligation on the cinemas not to show any film which "offends against good taste or decency".

THERE IS A VERY STRONG CASE FOR BELIEVING THAT THIS FILM SHOULD BE BANNED COMPLETELY.

Further information on any aspect of this matter may be obtained from:

The Nationwide Festival of Light, 21a Down Street, London, W1Y 7DN.

Tel: 01-499 5949

The director of the Festival of Light, Raymond Johnston, set the tone in an article on the film for the *Church of England Newspaper* on 23 November. 'Despite considerable skill in the visual field, the film is in the worst possible taste without quite toppling over into blasphemy. Its theme is sick, its story veering unsteadily between sadism and sheer silliness. It leaves a very nasty taste in the mouth. Though not in itself blasphemous, it will tend to discredit the New Testament story of Jesus in confused semi-pagan minds.' This did not prevent the *Church of England Newspaper*'s columnist Eddie Stride describing the film as 'cultural vandalism' on the same page.

Knowing that *Monty Python's Life of Brian* was certain to encounter protest, the film's distributors, CIC, decided to act cautiously: *Brian* would be launched in London in November and held there until after Christmas. This would give it a chance to establish

2

3. EVALUATION

(a) All reviewers agree that the film has many moments of genuine comedy:

"hysterically funny" - Daily Express
"magically funny....tremendously entertaining" - Daily Mail
"a very funny film" - Evening News
etc.

(b) Defenders of the film have pointed out that -

(i) It could be taken as "a comment on the times" (Ferman).
) It could be taken as "lampooning the Biblical epic" (Ferman).
) Brian himself is never a religious figure (Ferman).
The Monty Python team have a vast popular following (Ferman).
The Monty Python team have not tried or managed to insult direct (Daily Mail).
It is packing the U.S. cinemas in those areas where it has n banned, and is making a lot of money.

made against the film:

uses the set for Zeffirelli's TV Jesus of Nazareth.
parallel to the life of Jesus of Nazareth is so close
verage audience will take it as a parody.
here were no New Testament history of Jesus, the film
most of its point - it is a "film à clef".
tians are used to the parodying of Christian officers
ions - but this is different.
s a strong anti-Jewish theme in the burlesque
e population of 1st century Palestine.
ination of fanatical religious credulity, Messianic
life-pattern almost identical to that of Jesus and
e and display is precisely calculated to destroy
everence for the figure of the real Jesus in the
the most stalwart believers.
nce upon schoolchildren (if left with an 'AA'
ar olds can see it) will be especially damaging
eachers of religious education will be faced
blems:

esus tell people to f--- off?"
us have sex with girls like Brian in the film?"

ensive to practising Christians" (agreed by
ersation).
-year old child of mine to see it" (agreed
ritic in private conversation).
lm I have seen in 9 years of viewing"
of New York).
ety, U.S. media journal).
ds" (London Evening News).
he life and death of Christ" (National
pera about Auschwitz, with characters
lliam Buckley, U.S. critic).

3..

4. CRITICAL COMMENT (cont'd)

(h) "The film is blasphemous, sacrilegious and an incitement to possible violence. We have never come across such a foul, disgusting, blasphemous film before. Life of Brian is a vicious attack upon Judaism and the Bible and a cruel mockery of the religious feelings of Christians as well." (Rabbi Abraham Hecht, President of the Rabbinical Alliance of America).

5. ACTION

(a) All local authorities are responsible under the 1952 Cinematograph Act for the health and welfare of children under 16 in cinemas. They therefore have a duty imposed by Parliament which relates directly to the 14-16 year old children who may see this film if it is left with an 'AA' certificate. They would be liable at law if a court found that they had refused to consider the harm which could be caused by the showing of this film in the cinemas of their area for which they are the controlling licensing authority.

(b) Christians and Jews should therefore remind local authorities energetically of their statutory duty. They must insist on a preview. Cinemas will then recognise that before they show this film the local authority wishes it to be seen by the relevant committee.

(c) The viewing committee may come to one of three possible decisions:

(i) to leave the film with an 'AA' certificate and risk the consequences;

(ii) to change the certificate to 'X' - meaning only those over 18 may see the film; or

(iii) to ban the film entirely from the local cinemas.

(d) It should be stressed that a total ban on a violent or obscene film (which the B.B.F.C. has certificated) is not an unusual occurrence in a number of local authority areas, from industrial Yorkshire to Cornwall. Furthermore, the Home Office model licensing conditions, which most local authorities use when licensing cinemas annually, lay an obligation on the cinemas not to show any film which "offends against good taste or decency".

THERE IS A VERY STRONG CASE FOR BELIEVING THAT THIS FILM SHOULD BE BANNED COMPLETELY.

Further information on any aspect of this matter may be obtained from:
The Nationwide Festival of Light,
21a Down Street,
London, W1Y 7DN.

Tel: 01-499 5949

itself as the non-blasphemous entertainment it really was and to avoid any clashes with the church calendar. (When the film went on general release at the beginning of 1980 *Brian* was tactfully withdrawn over Easter.) But, as in America, the real battle would begin when the film went into the provinces.

As Chapter 3 pointed out, the usually accepted film censors in the United Kingdom do not have real control over what is shown in British cinemas. Power is held, not by the British Board of Film Censors, but the three-hundred-and-seventy or so local district councils who are the licensing authorities for the cinema buildings themselves. The practice has grown up by which local authorities make it a condition of their licences to cinemas that the cinemas abide by the certificates awarded by the BBFC, but the councils retain the powers to vary these conditions: they may decide to permit the showing of a film refused a certificate by the BBFC, they may refuse permission for a film passed by the BBFC to be shown, they may change the rating from the one awarded by the BBFC. During the 1960s the Greater London Council was prepared, on appeal, to permit the showing of films refused a certificate by the British Board of Film Censors, and was strongly criticized by Mrs Whitehouse and the Festival of Light for doing so. Following Mr Raymond Blackburn's successful prosecution on grounds of obscenity in 1975 of *More About the Language of Love*, a film the GLC had passed, the GLC has retreated from the liberal position it once held to one of conformity with the ratings of the Board.

Outside London, as *Monty Python's Life of Brian* was to show, the attitudes of local councils are entirely haphazard. Some councils have no committee with responsibility for film censorship, some have delegated the authority to a county committee representing several districts, some have no cinemas in their area anyway. Of the three-hundred-and-seventy district councils (including those with no cinemas) about seventy take an active interest in what is shown on the local screens, and of these about a dozen are known to be strict censors. If there is a geographical pattern, then the north tends to be stricter than the south. West Yorkshire, according to James Ferman, the Secretary of the BBFC, is 'the most heavily censored area in the English-speaking world – and that includes South Africa'.

The system of censorship is made even more haphazard by the way it is enforced. Given that a film has received a certificate from the British Board of Film Censors, it will, if booked, be seen in the local cinema – unless the district council, or rather the committee of district councillors responsible, issues a stop notice. The cinema may then appeal and request that the committee attends a viewing. After the viewing, which they *must* attend, the committee can decide to continue its ban, to lift it or to vary the BBFC's certificate, usually by raising the restrictive rating. The alteration of ratings (which includes changing the certificate shown at the beginning of the film) is a nuisance for the cinema, which must change all the advertising, and for the exhibitor, who must change the print of the film. CIC decided on a firm policy towards *Brian*: where a viewing was requested for a local council, they would arrange it, but they would not co-operate with local censorship. The British Board of Film Censors had rated the film 'AA' – if a local council decided that instead it should be 'X', CIC would refuse to show it. No attempt would be made to get round the ruling of the local council, by private free showings or by turning the cinema into a club. Thus *Brian* was kept out of many more areas by a locally imposed 'X' rating than by an outright ban.

The Festival of Light may have wished to 'avoid media coverage' but the media made this impossible. Hymn-singing protestors gathered outside the Plaza Cinema in Lower Regent Street for the première on 8 November. On 9 November in the Synod of the Church of England the Chairman, the Archbishop of York, Dr Stuart Blanch, interrupted business to make a solemn statement:

> The film *The Life of Brian* has just opened in London. I have not seen it, and I suppose I am unlikely to do so. However, members will have seen the reviews and will be aware that there is a great deal of concern throughout the country about it. For the immediate future, it will be up to Christian people and others who share this concern to ensure that in this case, as in other cases where it seems that a film has been made which devalues humanity, in their own areas the local viewing committee is alerted to the need to see the film before it is publicly shown and, having done so, to take responsible decisions as to whether and on what conditions it should be shown.

The Archbishop's appeal was heard, for the Church of England Board for Social Responsibility began to circulate anti-*Brian* material from the Festival of Light. In the months to come the Bishops of Durham, Bath and Wells, Chichester, Birmingham, Chester, Derby and Worcester all protested against the film: but the protest that is best remembered is the television debate with the Bishop of Southwark, Mervyn Stockwood, and Malcolm Muggeridge on one side, and John Cleese and Michael Palin on the other. Ten years after Muggeridge's religious programme gave way to *Monty Python's Flying Circus*, the alternative forms of late-night entertainment came face to face before the audience of *Friday Night, Saturday Morning*.

It was John Cleese who remarked during the confrontation on the night of 9 November that the scene was like a Python sketch. The chat show began affably enough, with Cleese and Palin talking on their own to their host, Tim Rice – himself the lyricist of *Jesus Christ, Superstar*. But while a second clip from the film was being shown, Stockwood and Muggeridge came on to the set. The full effect of the entry of the Bishop in his sweeping purple cassock and chunky cross (his normal working dress) was missed by the television audience, who found him already seated beside a bronzed and gleaming Malcolm Muggeridge when the film excerpt ended. Tim Rice explained that Stockwood and Muggeridge had seen the film earlier in the day and invited their comments. With that, the gloves were off.

The two Pythons were rather taken aback by the virulence of the attack: all four had met before the programme began and there was no hint of what was to come. For their part the Pythons remained courteous and restrained. They also tried to control the studio audience, who showed signs of partisanship on their behalf. It may be their evident seniority in years that made Stockwood and Muggeridge appear patronizing. Stockwood drew a laugh with his reference to undergraduate humour; Muggeridge spoke wearily of the ease with which the Pythons were able to extract humour from the most solemn of mysteries. The Bishop's most telling point was that without the existence of Jesus the film would not have been made, and he ignored the Pythons' protestations that the film was (where it treated of religion) about the distortions of faith, not faith itself. Muggeridge concentrated on what he saw as the Pythons' mockery of the incarnation, God made manifest as Man, the inspiration of Art and Civilization, though Cleese pointed out some of the less civilized events and institutions Christianity had been associated with. Stockwood was most upset by the treatment of the crucifixion, for he could not separate what Christian iconography has made of the method of execution from its historical context as a

Roman punishment. The crucifix is the most potent Christian symbol; the ultimate shock of *Monty Python's Life of Brian* is that it ends with mass execution and a song that laughs at death.

As the discussion lengthened, Palin and Cleese found it harder to remain polite, particularly as their opponents made it difficult for them to get a word in. It is worth repeating John Cleese's explanation of the film; it is about 'closed systems of thought, whether they are political or theological or religious or whatever; systems by which whatever evidence is given to a person he merely adapts it, fits it into his ideology'. *Friday Night, Saturday Morning* was a genuine confrontation, but it was not a genuine debate, far less so than the argument with ABC TV in a New York court. This was not because of Cleese or Palin, who were quite ready to explain their actions, but the fierce attitude from the other side. Viewers will long remember Bishop Stockwood's parting shot, assuring the Pythons they would get their thirty pieces of silver.

Although *The Life of Brian* was not due to go on general release until after Christmas, *Friday Night, Saturday Morning* alerted local pressure groups to what was coming. At the British Board of Film Censors James Ferman has instituted the practice of sending district councils a review of the films it has seen and an explanation of the Board's decisions about them. The review of *Brian* went out of its way to stress the film's innocence:

Not only does the film make clear that Brian could not reasonably be taken to be a caricature of Jesus Christ, but the Christian faith itself is in no way maligned.   Nor could the script really be described as containing "any contemptuous, reviling, scurrilous or ludicrous matter relating to God, Jesus Christ, the Bible, or the formularies of the Church of England as by law established," which is the legal formulation of blasphemy given in Article 214 of Stephen's Digest of the Criminal Law, 9th edition (1950).   Such ludicrous matter as the film does contain relates only <u>indirectly</u> to matters of religion, while concerning itself with comic lay figures wholly without religious significance.   Lawyers were consulted on the question of the film's possible blasphemy, particularly in the light of the recent <u>Gay News</u> case, but there seems no parallel here for the elements which made the poem in that case so profoundly offensive to some Christians.   This film treats the Bible not in religious terms, but as an essential part of our common cultural history.   The nativity as here portrayed leaves St Luke unscathed, while lampooning the cliches of Hollywood's biblical epics and of countless commercial Christmas cards.   Monty Python's usual schoolboy humour is here let loose on a period of history appropriately familiar to every schoolboy in the West, and a faith which could be shaken by such good-humoured ribaldry would be a very precarious faith indeed.

In its covering commentary the BBFC warned local councillors that the response of some of them to 'advance reports both alarmist and beside the point suggests that some local licensing committees may be exercising their statutory powers without sufficient care and attention to the real issues involved'.

For the citizens of Harrogate, West Yorkshire, the warning came too late, for the Borough Council's film selection sub-committee had already banned the film unseen. The Borough Council had acquired its censorship powers as a result of local government reorganization in 1975; since then the sub-committee had issued 267 stop notices: of these they viewed forty-five films following appeal, approving twenty-eight and banning eighteen. Though assiduous in its work, it turns out that the sub-committee was not as watchful as it should be: in May 1979 they issued a stop notice on *The Warriors*, only to discover that the film had already been shown in Harrogate. The same thing happened in February 1980 with *Beneath the Valley of the Ultra-Vixens*. The Harrogate councillors who decided to act against *Brian* were among the first to

respond to the Festival of Light's appeal for local action, but local reaction proved equally strong. Fellow Councillor Cecil Margolis described the four-man sub-committee's ban as 'a denial of liberty and a rejection of human rights', and the main General Purposes Committee decided that *Brian* should at least be previewed. By eight votes to four the ban was upheld, though the local debate continued. Harrogate District Trades Council condemned the committee's decision as 'a violation of the rights of expression and freedom of thought', but committee chairman Councillor Harold Hitchen stood by the system of local censorship: 'It works and we intend to fight for it.' Prevented from seeing *Brian* in Harrogate, all the determined filmgoer had to do was drive seventeen miles south to Leeds, or eighteen miles west to York. In March 1981 Harrogate Borough Council voted to scrap its film censorship powers.

In Surrey, censorship operated on a different arrangement: there are eleven district councils in the county, of which five retain their licensing powers (and had no objections to *Brian*) but the other seven

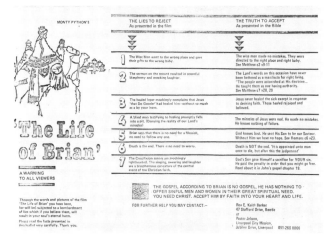

delegate the decision to a joint committee. Two of these districts, Runnymede and Mole Valley have no cinemas in their area, but still send two members to the committee. These two joined Guildford, Tandridge, Surrey Heath, Epsom and Spelthorne in excluding the film. After viewing *Brian* on 24 January 1980 the councillors decided that the film could be shown but only with an 'X' certificate. In line with its policy, CIC declined to show the film in their area. Similar joint committees kept *Brian* out of Hereford and parts of Berkshire, where the County Council Public Protection Committee decided that *Brian* was unsafe. The most thorough ban, however, came from the Association of District Councils of Cornwall. When the now customary protests forced a viewing of the film on 25 February, seventeen members of the Cornish panel viewed *Brian* at the Truro Plaza. Afterwards eight voted for a ban and eight voted against; the casting vote against *Brian* came from the chairman. One panel member had no doubts: 'All the people in the film should be locked up in Broadmoor. It's twenty years since I have been to the cinema, but if that is what is shown I shall not go again.'

Brian did badly in the West Country. In East Devon the district council for Sidmouth and Exmouth banned the film without seeing it, on the grounds, according to one councillor, that 'You don't have to see a pigsty to know that it stinks.' A formal application from a Sidmouth cinema, however, meant that the Environmental Services Committee was obliged to see it; their demand for an 'X' rating kept *Brian* away. *Brian*'s unpopularity in the West Country was partly the result of a joint letter urging a ban sent to all councils in Avon and Somerset by the Bishop of Bath and Wells, the Roman Catholic Bishop of Clifton, the Chairman of the Bristol Methodists and the local Moderator of the United Reformed Church. Though several councils in the area decided to ask for an 'X', Bristol made no ruling, while special coach trips brought deprived fans from Cornwall and East Devon to Exeter, where the film did excellent business for several weeks.

On the south coast Thanet District Council's Conservative-controlled General Purposes Committee banned *Brian* sight unseen, and so enraged the management of the Carlton Cinema in Margate and the nearby Chippy Fish and Chip Shop that they both decided to ban anti-*Brian* councillors from their doors. Two independent councillors forced a debate on the issue by the full council, while petitions protesting against the ban were circulated. Demonstrators interrupted the debate and the committee agreed to view the film. Reversing its decision by eleven votes to three, it sent a recommendation that *Brian* be seen as an 'AA' to be ratified by the whole council. Across the Thames Estuary at Southend, an anti-*Brian* petition from the Free Churches of Southend and Festival of Light material quoted in committee persuaded the

Environmental Health Committee to order an 'X' rating, but when the film appeared without trouble in neighbouring Basildon they agreed to see the film. Following a debate in full council, *Brian* got its 'AA'. In Swansea, however, a special meeting (costing a reported £350 in attendance allowances) upheld by twenty-two votes to fifteen the council's Public Protection Committee's decision to ban the film. *Monty Python and the Holy Grail* was shown instead. Shrewsbury and Atcham decided to ask for an 'X' rating, but when they learned this would mean that the film would not be shown, settled for an 'AA'.

In Scotland *Brian* met no difficulties in Edinburgh, but was 'X' rated in Glasgow, where councillors attending the viewing were handed nails by the militantly Protestant and anti-Communist Pastor Jack Glass as they walked into the cinema. (Later, the rating was changed to 'AA'.) In Belfast an 'X' rating kept *Brian* away, but there were no difficulties in Londonderry. On the Isle of Man it was the protestor who suffered, for a Baptist Minister was taken to court for handing out leaflets protesting at *Brian* outside a Douglas cinema in contravention of a local by-law. The Reverend Matthew F. Else was conditionally discharged for one year.

Up and down the country the examples multiply, with one council thrown into uproar, while a mile or so away *Brian* was shown without even a preview being called for. By the time the film had completed its general circuit release councillors from over a hundred towns and districts had had a free trip to *The Life of Brian*. In the end ten decisions to ban outright were taken (though that included the decision for the whole of Cornwall) but twenty-seven districts and district associations insisted on an 'X' rating which kept *Brian* from their areas. The case of *Monty Python's Life of Brian* seems intended to demonstrate the wisdom of the conclusion reached by the Committee on Obscenity and Film Censorship, set up by the Home Office under the chairmanship of Professor Bernard Williams. Their report was published in November 1979, just as *Brian*'s troubles began. Commenting on the variations and vagaries of local censorship, the Williams report concluded:

> We cannot believe that local attitudes and *mores* vary to the extent that these differing decisions imply; dissenting decisions are often confined to the area of one particular local authority, are not consistent throughout a given region of the country, and are not shared by neighbouring authorities. We believe that a system in which local censorship means that people wishing to see a particular film have to travel a few extra miles to the next town simply brings ridicule to the system with no compensating advantages. The majority of our witnesses seemed to be of the same view and we conclude that the possession by local

authorities of the power to control the films shown locally cannot be justified by any local variation in taste and opinion.

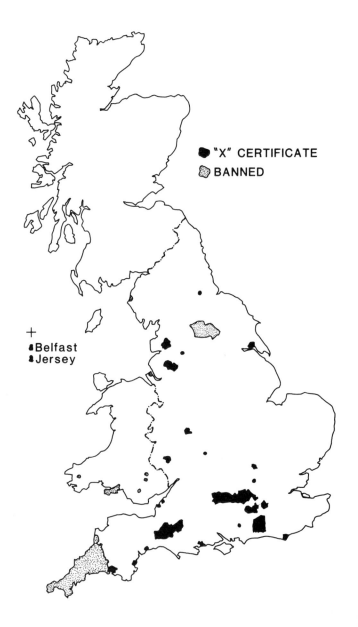

⬤ "X" CERTIFICATE
🔘 BANNED

+
▲ Belfast
▲ Jersey

The Williams committee has recommended that local censorship in the United Kingdom should be ended, and the system unified by the establishment of a statutory body to take over the functions of the BBFC.

Meanwhile the United Kingdom box office receipts of *Monty Python's Life of Brian* have been put at £4 million.

Besides Britain, Canada and the United States, thirteen other countries have seen *The Life of Brian*. France, Spain and Belgium, where the Roman Catholic Church has strong traditional influence, have remained generally unperturbed. The film has not been seen in Italy, but this may be because of the language problem as much as any caution about the opinion of the Holy See. In Ireland there is no language problem, but there also seems to be no chance that *Brian* will be shown. No exhibitor has tried to get the film past the Republic's strict Film Censorship Act. What would happen if he did is shown by the fate of the LP featuring the sound-track of the film.

All was well until, on 15 January 1980, the *Irish Independent* picked up the story and headlined 'Blasphemy Beats the Censor'. Father Brian D'Arcy, known in Ireland as 'the showbiz priest', was quoted as saying that the film (which he had not seen) was blasphemous: 'Anybody who buys the record and finds it funny must have something wrong with their mentality.' Two days after the story broke, the Dublin firm distributing the record announced that it was not importing any more *Brian* records – because they were getting threatening phone calls. 'We decided that it would be for the best to drop further distribution. It was not worth all the hassle.' Threatening phone calls, Father

Brian and the *Irish Independent* closed a loophole in the Irish censorship laws, for records and tapes are not under the jurisdiction of the Republic's Censorship of Publications Board. (The *Scrapbook* was not banned, but retailers handled it with reluctance.) The same loophole allows video-tape cassettes and, barring the activities of censorious customs officers, for the moment technology remains ahead of the law.

In South Africa the loopholes are more tightly closed. The 1974 Publications Act controls 'any publication or object, film, public entertainment or intended public entertainment' and subjects them all to the same restrictions. Section 47 covers, almost in the same breath, matters of indecency, obscenity, blasphemy and anything that brings 'inhabitants of the Republic into ridicule or contempt', is 'prejudicial to the safety of the state' or 'discloses with reference to any judicial proceedings'. The only chink in this armour is that books are able to circulate in the country until such time as they are banned, and the enterprising publisher or distributor hopes to sell as many copies as possible before the ban is imposed. The Pythons have long been regarded as prejudicial to the state of South Africa, for *Monty Python's Big Red Book* and the *Bok* were quickly placed on *Jacobsen's Index of Objectionable Literature*. On 18 January the *Brian* book joined the distinguished (and undistinguished) company of the banned.

Life for Africa, A (The Story of Bram Fischer)	Naomi Mitchison			2480	4111	21.12.73
Life Full of Holes, A	Driss Ben Hamed Charhadi			454	1407	25.3.66
Life Long Love	Rennie MacAndrew			1510	5730	17.8.56
Life of an Amorous Woman, The (and other Writings)	Ihara Saikaku			157	1018	5.2.65
Life of Brian, The/Scrapbook of Brian of Nazareth	Monty Python	(a) + (b)		139	6810	18.1.80
Life of Korean Women, The	Li Jung Sook					
Life of Passion	Gordon Temple			1510	5730	17.8.56
Life of the Metal Worker's in the Rumanian People's Republic, The (Published by the Central Council of Trade Unions of the Rumanian People's Republic Bucharest, 1964)						
Life of the Workers in New China (September, 1963)		(1)		1510	5730	17.8.56
Life of Tilly Lagourd, The	Jules Jean Morac			1510	5730	17.8.56
Life Romance (October, 1952)		(1)		1510	5730	17.8.56

Reg.-nr. 66793   Fabr.-nr.

Rekvirent: . Syncron Film   Antall ekspl.: 1
Filmfabrikk: .   eng.
Filmens norsk titel: Profeten Brians liv og historie (Monty Python Life of Brian)
(Denne tittel må brukes ved forevisningen)   Dram. WS farger

Filmens lengde før klipning: 2558 meter; etter klipning: meter.
Kontrollavgift betalt med kr. 1482.-
Denne film godkjennes ikke til forevisning offentlig i Norge.

Anmerkninger:

STATENS FILMKONTROLL

Oslo, den 14.jan.1980

Innhold: Skildring av Brian - født samtidig med Kristus i "nabostallen". Blir tilslutt korsfestet. .

Greece, Israel, Austria, Switzerland, Holland, West Germany, Denmark and Sweden accepted *Brian* without comment. (In Israel fleeting snatches of *Monty Python's Flying Circus* had appeared in the locally produced satire programme *Nikui Rosh*, itself the subject of much criticism from Israel's righteous.) In Australia there was a flurry in Queensland when the state's Films Board of Review accepted the Commonwealth Film Censorship Board's 'M' rating (= mature audiences, fifteen years and over). Though in practice censorship operates on a commonwealth basis, as in Canada the individual states have their own powers to control films, and Queensland's Films Board of Review takes a much tougher line than the other states. However, the Board took the view that it did not have the power to ban films offensive to the religious, much to the annoyance of Roman Catholic Father Gerry Nichol who watched the film with the censors and recommended a ban. The decision led to questions in the State Parliament, but although the Minister for Culture agreed that *Brian* was 'grubby and tasteless' and said that Queensland had a duty to discourage the proliferation of such films, he confirmed that the Board was within its rights. *The Life of Brian* has become one of the ten most successful films ever at the box office in Australia.

As early as December 1979 Syncron-Film in Oslo had snapped up the rights to exhibit *Brian* in Norway (with sub-titles). The film was submitted in the normal way to the Norwegian censors, a board of five civil servants working under the Ministry of Justice. When the film was viewed it had not been released in either Sweden or Denmark, but there were plentiful reports of the trouble *Brian* had caused in Britain and the United States. Locally, a pythonesque Norwegian television comedy show, *Press*, had recently caused an uproar with a cookery sketch on how to feed five thousand people with five loaves and two fishes. To Syncron-Film's complete astonishment the censors unanimously decided to ban *Brian*.

Since this was the first time the Norwegian censors had ever banned a comedy, Syncron-Film asked the censors for their reasons. These were a month in coming, but it turned out that while the censors may not have held religious views themselves (their chairman, Mrs Else Germeten, has admitted that she does not) they felt it was necessary to protect the religious sensitivities of others. The closing mass execution was the main reason for the ban, but the Sermon on the Mount was also unacceptable. Syncron-Film began a campaign of press showings and there followed a general uproar. In Sweden *The Life of Brian* went on release with the warning: 'This film is so funny that it is banned in Norway.'

All this was very embarrassing to the film censors, all the more so because their offices are three floors above those of Syncron-Film, in the same building, and the two sides kept meeting in the lift. They both started to look for a compromise. The censors explained that they had jurisdiction only over the film images, not over the sound. Could Syncron-Film possibly black out the last scene, but run the song? For their part, Syncron-Film cut the film to a form acceptable to the censors, but they then had to get the agreement of the Pythons. Terry Jones flew to Oslo and watched an uncensored screening at the American Embassy, crowded with British Embassy staff who had heard about the film. Terry Jones promised to put the case for accepting cuts to the Pythons when he returned to London. (Syncron-Film were so keen to show the film that they wanted to buy the Norwegian rights outright.) But the Pythons stuck to their position, the film must not be cut.

Six months later, the Pythons heard that *Monty Python's Life of Brian* (with Norwegian sub-titles) was running in Oslo. A quiet compromise had been reached: the film and English soundtrack remained untouched, only some of the dialogue remained untranslated in the sub-titles. Many Norwegians speak English.

It was the Pythons who showed that it is possible to dispense with punchlines, and *Monty Python: the Case Against* does not try to invent one, for the Pythons, and those who would censor them, are still hard at work. The struggle between those who draw the line and those whose punchlines cross it is still going on. This book has tried to show how various the means of censorship are and how variable their application can be. It has also shown how frequently and ludicrously people have tried to stop things being said with only the vaguest notion of what those things are. Some form of protection for the young seems necessary, to shield them from images of violence and sex which adults may deliberately seek out, whether they are forbidden or not. Adults must be free to choose. The censorship of ideas and information is always unnecessary, and dangerous.

The Pythons have a comic commitment to challenge accepted views of how things are, including the role of authority. Those who oppose them have an ideological commitment to preserving the authority that prevents such challenges being made. Some forms of censorship are established by law, their rules are known and the activities of those who operate them are open. But much of the pressure on the Pythons has been unofficial, private censorship of various kinds, both commercial and institutional. These pressures are far harder to resist because they are implicit, not explicit, and cannot be challenged openly because they do not operate in the open. But even with open censorship, the question must always be asked: who is censoring the censors?

It was suggested at the beginning of this book that when a society decides to draw the line, it is describing a line around its own culture. When *Monty Python's Flying Circus* was transmitted in Japan in 1976 the 'Ministry of Silly Walks' was not shown for fear of offending traditional Japanese respect for those in authority. In Britain ministries are fair game, but royalty is taboo. *The Life of Brian* shows that while the religious may be in a minority in the United Kingdom and America, they hold very firmly to their beliefs. In Britain the link between religion and the state is still strong, as the *Gay News* trial shows; but it is only Christianity that is protected from blasphemy by fines and prison sentences. (Recent proposals on the law of blasphemy may change this.) In both Britain and the United States conservative religious views go hand in hand with conservative political beliefs, and local politicians and clergy have been seen hand in hand exercising censorship.

The singing victims of the mass crucifixion at the close of *The Life of Brian* are deeply offensive to committed Christians who have taken Christ's passion and death on the cross as a statement of sacrifice and redemption: 'He died that we might live.' In this respect, the Pythons cannot be said to have undermined their faith; if anything they have strengthened

it. But what is revealing about the episode is not the response to the mockery of religion (which the Pythons deny) but the mockery of death. Death, far more than religion, seems to be the twentieth-century taboo, as the Pythons discovered early on with the 'Undertakers' sketch. Silly sex and comic violence, the mere use of words, are not threats to society, and society has learned to tolerate them, but death is more problematic. To which the Pythons reply:

> Always look on the bright side of life . . .
> For life is quite absurd
> And death's the final word
> You must always face the curtain with a bow
> Forget about your sin – give the audiences a grin
> Enjoy it – it's your last chance anyhow.

On the other side of the line, the Python method has pushed film and television comedy in a multiplicity of directions, and not just those to do with giving offence, which the subject of this book must needs over-emphasize. In Britain *Not the Nine O'Clock News*, and in America *Saturday Night Live*, have been able to hit the targets they have chosen because of the precedent set by *Monty Python*.

The Python method that takes all things to the Absurd has been their best protection against would-be censors. The role of 'licensed jesters' is a traditional one that has always allowed things to be said in comedy which would be impermissible as serious art, let alone as a direct political statement. And the great example of the Pythons has been to show that if they are licensed jesters, then they have owned the licence themselves. As the ABC TV case shows, financial control always outweighs creative control. Though no Python is complaining of poverty, the Pythons have always been prepared to put their profits on the line. Ironically, this has usually made their ventures more, not less, profitable. Many businessmen fail to understand Python principles – the ultimate absurdity was an offer from America to buy the 'format' of the Python shows, that is, *Monty Python* without the Pythons – corporate methods do not have the conceptual framework to deal with an anarchist collective, run by intelligent and arrogant comedians who have proved that their method works.

It is not wise to predict where the Python method will take them next, although plans have been laid for another film. There is a striking resemblance between the six Pythons and the six squabbling heroes of Terry Gilliam's latest film (with a Michael Palin script), *The Time Bandits*. Randall is spokesman and leader, but the others are always pleading with him to do something; Vermin loves ordure, Strutter has a cynical style, Wally keeps the peace, Og says nothing and Fidget always wants to do things differently. Slipping between the conventions of time and place, there is no telling where they will turn up next.

The experience of the Pythons has been to underline the principle that you should never leave your values to the state, for there are plenty of people who are keen to make the state's values theirs, and not yours. Censorship is a means of keeping systems closed. Eric Idle has written,

> At least one way of measuring the freedom of any society is the amount of comedy that is permitted, and clearly a healthy society permits more satirical comment than a repressive, so that if comedy is to function in some way as a safety release then it must obviously deal with these taboo areas. This is part of the responsibility we accord our licensed jesters, that nothing be excused the searching light of comedy. If anything can survive the probe of humour it is clearly of value, and conversely all groups who claim immunity from laughter are claiming special privileges which should not be granted.

Terry Gilliam sums it up (of course) differently. He told *Playboy*: 'We've got to maintain a certain level of offence; otherwise, we're just entertainers. It's one way of proving to ourselves that we're not just in it for the money.'

82 Fetter Lane
EC4
In the City of London

Robert Hewison

Chris — this should read OK. provided it's big enough

Acknowledgements

The author is very grateful to the following for assistance, information
or material for quotation and reproduction: *Peter Bennett,*
BBC Audience Research Unit, ~~~~ *Graham Chapman,*
John Cleese, Alison Davies, Denton Hall & Burgin, James Ferman,
Canon J.A.Fisher, *Jill Foster,* Cathryn Game, Terry Gilliam, John Gledhill,
J.J.Goldberg, John Goldstone, Roger Hancock, Hendrik Hertzberg,
Chris Holgate, Eric Idle, John Jacobsen, Anne James, Kim 'Howard' Johnson,
Raymond Johnston, Terry Jones, Ian MacNaughton, John Mortimer,
Michael Palin, Jackie Parker, B.J.Pegler, Julian Porter, Michael Rubinstein,
John Savage, Geoffrey Strachan, Roydon Thomas, Nicolas Walter,
F.D.Wardle, and Mike Watts.

— *1 line #* —

The words of Sir Hugh Greene are quoted from *The Third Floor Front:
A View of Broadcasting in the Sixties* (Bodley Head, London, 1969);
Lord Hill is quoted from *Behind the Screen: The Broadcasting Memoirs
of Lord Hill* (Sidgwick & Jackson, London, 1974); Mrs Mary Whitehouse
is quoted from *Who Does She Think She Is?* (New English Library, London,
1972), *Mary Whitehouse* by Max Caulfield (Mowbrays, London, 1975),
and *Whitehouse* by Michael Tracey and David Morrison (Macmillan, London,
1979). Roger Wilmut's *From Fringe to Flying Circus* (Eyre Methuen, London,
1980) is an invaluable guide to British comedy since 1960.

— *1 line #* —

*Stills from Monty Python's Flying Circus, Monty Python and the Holy
Grail, The Life of Brian and other Python images reproduced
by kind permission of Python Productions Ltd.*

— *1 line #* —

> *Copy (A)*

Other photographs by kind permission of the following: p. 25 Radio Times;
p. 38 Python (Monty) Pictures Ltd and Drew Mara; p. 70 David Redfern;
p. 79 Kim Howard Johnson; p. 93 Syncron-Film; p. 94 HandMade Films; back
cover: rubber stamp based on a photograph by Roger Last.

Material quoted from BBC archives remains the copyright of the BBC.